"Enter this book at your own risk. It's loaded with knock-down humor that reveals a woman's thoughts with the same clarity as a makeup mirror. And here's what else I love: The insights are straight from Anita's priceless heart."

—PATSY CLAIRMONT, Women of Faith speaker;
author of *All Cracked Up*

"Anita Renfroe is the same on and off the stage and in the pages of this book: funny but with great heart. She makes the everyday comical, the mundane laughable, and relationships hysterical. Thanks for always making me laugh, Anita!"

—DONNA VANLIERE, *New York Times*
best-selling author of THE CHRISTMAS HOPE series

if it's not
one thing
it's your
m*ther

Anita Renfroe

NAVPRESS®

BRINGING TRUTH TO LIFE

OUR GUARANTEE TO YOU

We believe so strongly in the message of our books that we are making this quality guarantee to you. If for any reason you are disappointed with the content of this book, return the title page to us with your name and address and we will refund to you the list price of the book. To help us serve you better, please briefly describe why you were disappointed. Mail your refund request to: NavPress, P.O. Box 35002, Colorado Springs, CO 80935.

The Navigators is an international Christian organization. Our mission is to advance the gospel of Jesus and His kingdom into the nations through spiritual generations of laborers living and discipling among the lost. We see a vital movement of the gospel, fueled by prevailing prayer, flowing freely through relational networks and out into the nations where workers for the kingdom are next door to everywhere.

NavPress is the publishing ministry of The Navigators. The mission of NavPress is to reach, disciple, and equip people to know Christ and make Him known by publishing life-related materials that are biblically rooted and culturally relevant. Our vision is to stimulate spiritual transformation through every product we publish.

ISBN 1-57683-993-1

Cover design by Terra Peterson, Bill Chiaravalle, Brand Navigation LLC
Cover photo by Don Jones Photography LLC
Creative Team: Terry Behimer, Traci Mullins, Darla Hightower, Arvid Wallen, Pat Reinheimer

Some of the anecdotal illustrations in this book are true to life and are included with the permission of the persons involved. All other illustrations are composites of real situations, and any resemblance to people living or dead is coincidental.

Published in association with the literary agency of Alive Communications, Inc., 7680 Goddard Street, Suite 200, Colorado Springs, Colorado, 80920 (www.alivecommunications.com)

Unless otherwise identified, all Scripture quotations in this publication are taken from the *THE MESSAGE* (MSG). Copyright © 1993, 1994, 1995, 1996, 2000, 2001, 2002. Used by permission of NavPress Publishing Group. Other versions used include: the HOLY BIBLE: NEW INTERNATIONAL VERSION® (NIV®). Copyright © 1973, 1978, 1984 by International Bible Society, used by permission of Zondervan Publishing House, all rights reserved; *The Living Bible* (TLB), copyright © 1971, used by permission of Tyndale House Publishers, Inc., Wheaton, IL 60189, all rights reserved.

Renfroe, Anita, 1962-
   If it's not one thing, it's your mother / by Anita Renfroe.
      p. cm.
   ISBN 1-57683-993-1
   1. Motherhood--Religious aspects--Christianity. 2. Mothers
--Religious aspects--Christianity. 3. Motherhood--Humor.
4. Mothers--Humor.   I. Title.
BV4529.18.R46 2006
248.8'431--dc22

2006010875

Printed in the United States of America
1 2 3 4 5 6 / 10 09 08 07 06

FOR A FREE CATALOG OF
NAVPRESS BOOKS & BIBLE STUDIES,
CALL 1-800-366-7788 (USA)
OR 1-800-839-4769 (CANADA)

the mother of all
tables of contents

A Word from My Daughter 7

Official Disclaimer 11

Chapter 1 No Wonder They Call It "Labor" 17

Chapter 2 A Little Mayo with the Momwich 29

Chapter 3 Stretch Marks 37

Chapter 4 Baby Books and Other Blueprints 47

Chapter 5 Eat This, You'll Feel Better 55

Chapter 6 It Came from Hollywood 63

Chapter 7 Actual Results May Vary 75

Chapter 8 All I Really Want 83

Chapter 9 Playing Favorites 89

Chapter 10 Moms of the Bible 97

Chapter 11 Other Mothers 103

Chapter 12 Utter Momsense 113

Chapter 13 Eating Your Young 121

Chapter 14 The Land Mine of All Holidays 129

Chapter 15 Smotherly Love 137

Chapter 16   The Mama Drama   147

Chapter 17   Mental Acreage   155

Chapter 18   The Mother of Invention   163

Chapter 19   Mom's Top 10   173

Chapter 20   Returning to the Mother Ship   183

Chapter 21   So Which One of Us Is Crazy?   191

A Word from My Mother   201

Acknowledgments   204

About the Author   206

a word
from
my daughter

(Author's note: I did not pay my daughter to write this, but I might add that she's young and will probably be needing some wheels soon. You may want to take that into account when reading the following.)

I've been going to women's events with my mom since before I had hips or bosoms. I've stood behind her product table helping women decide what they should take home with them. It is a private joke between my mom and me that several women will ALWAYS ask me, "Is your mom this funny at home?" I smile, look at my mom, and never really know how to answer that. To me, she's funnier offstage than on, but NO ONE seems funny when they are threatening to ground you. So until I figure out a politically correct way to say that, I just smile. If you come by my mom's table, think up another question, please!

It never ceases to amaze us how different we truly are. The most obvious example of this is seen in our clothing. My mom expresses her feelings by wearing colorful, funky, and *different* clothes. I, on the other hand, prefer a more classic look. Black and white catches my attention more than any vibrant color. I am more of an Ann Taylor kind of girl, whereas she frequents Chico's.

When I was around twelve years old I said to my mother, "You're not very mom-ish." She was, to say the least, taken aback. Those few words, I have learned, will most likely follow me throughout the remainder of my youth and into my adult life. To my mind, it didn't seem to be a degrading remark; I was just observing how she was never the bake-brownies-or-carpool-the-kids kind of mom. Her biggest fear wasn't that we would fall in with the wrong crowd or not go to the right college; it was that we would end up on Jerry Springer.

In our household, dinner is *loud.* I like to say it's the best free entertainment you will *ever* find. Now, I should warn you that if ever you come to our home for a dining experience, it's really more like the Verbal Olympics. I remember a couple of years ago when my eldest brother invited one of his friends over for dinner for the first time. Tim comes from a little more quiet and keep-to-themselves kind of family. So when we all sat down to eat and the laughing and yelling so you could talk over the person next to you began, he was a bit overwhelmed. He stopped us all in a rather impolite manner, but we're used to it, so, because he was a guest, we waited patiently to hear what the new guy had to say.

"Has it occurred to anyone here that no one is *listening*?"

Listening and talking in our house aren't mutually exclusive; we can do both at the same time. It's most likely a gift we received from our mother at a very young age. So, if you do stop by for dinner, consider yourself warned.

We are constantly laughing and that is one of the gifts of having a humorous mom. And you could never fault her for not being one of the most genuine people you've ever met. She's instilled in me many more-than-valuable insights that I will always treasure. It's truly a blessing to have a mother so wise that when she speaks, you listen. As you read this book you will come to find out my mom is hysterical, but also a woman who puts God before anything and anyone.

I think she's incredible. As cliché as it may sound, I want to be the kind of woman and mother she's been to myself and my brothers — mom-ish or not.

I love you so much, Mom!

Your favorite daughter,

Elypse

official
* disclaimer

S ee—here's the problem.
        Nobody knows.

I mean *NO*body. Not the scholars, not the theologians, not the philosophers, not the doctors or lawyers—NOBODY.

The subject of all this un-knowledge?

How motherhood was supposed to be *before* the first mom was evicted from paradise. You know, that singular moment when the perfect woman in the perfect garden with the perfect husband and perfect relationship with God messed it all up for everyone forever and ever. It just doesn't seem fair that we'll never really know what the plan for propagation of the species was *supposed* to look like under the original, perfect plan.

Sure, sure, we all know the verses in Genesis where part of the judgment of humankind for disobeying God was that childbirth would forever be difficult and full of pain, but what might it have been like otherwise? No epidural required . . . Could Eve have been waltzing through the Garden of Eden one day and pushed back a cabbage leaf to find a beautiful baby, fully potty trained? Or maybe the stork would have been the delivery agent of a teenager who already knew how to drive and had respectful regard for his parents. Could we have enjoyed raising our children without colic, immunizations, butterfly stitches, questionable report cards, or suspiciously missing cookies from the cookie jar? Could motherhood have been a relationship devoid of layers of complications and conflicted emotions and unresolved angst from our own childhoods and blame and guilt and struggle?

Truth is—we'll never know.

Thus we are left with what motherhood is—a strange concoction of love, protection, pain, closeness, separation, guessing, guilt, pride, duty, sacrifice, hormones, heartache, and hilarity. We have all had some relationship with motherhood, as we have all had one—(not necessarily your birth mother, but an adopted one, a grandmother or aunt who was your mother figure, or another woman who decided to mother you without your particular consent)—and some of us *are* one. I would fall into the category of having one and being one.

First, I was a daughter.

I was a daughter a long time before I was a mother.

And I've had a mother longer than I've been a mother.

I love my mother and my daughter, and I am well loved by them both.

I am not a psychologist. Anything said in this book that seems the least bit psychological, I probably made it up. Anything that seems psycho is all me.

I am not a theologian. I have friends who are and, believe me, I know the difference. I do love God and I love His Word, the Bible. I love the women in the Bible because they are not airbrushed to moral supermodel perfection, but glowing in their imperfectness, which gives us all reason to hope. Anything that seems like a theological statement is more than likely just my opinion. I attempt to avoid straight-up heresy, but please do not write me lengthy e-mail treatises rebutting my views on women in the Bible. I am a comedian. I am a belly button in the Body of Christ, not a frontal lobe.

I do feel that I have a unique perspective on the Mother/Daughter Thing. We have a 60/40/Teen cloister of women in our household. My mom is in her sixties, I am in my forties, and my daughter is in her teens. The amount of teenage and midlife hormones floating in the air is almost a visible fog. This means that every day is like the movie *The Perfect Storm*—all the elements exist for the convergence of three very powerful forces to make something emotionally devastating. Each day that it doesn't happen is pretty much a miracle.

I am a daughter. Anything that I said in this book that makes my mom look like a great woman is probably true. Anything that I said in this book that makes my mom look like a flawed human being is probably true, too. But it's never meant to dishonor her. Mom, I love you and so much admire all the pain you have walked through in your life. You have honored God with your life through it all and always tried to do what was right to the best of your ability. The way you believe that God uses families and the gifts He has put in all of our family will be your lasting legacy. You might get the Five Stars for Legendary Service from your company but your rewards in eternity will probably be innumerable.

I am also a mother to one of the most amazing future-women that God has ever dreamed up. My daughter is brilliant and beautiful in all ways externally and internally and will no doubt accomplish things I can only imagine. She has emotional intelligence and wisdom beyond her years—due, in part, to my excellent motherhood, I'm sure. (I am also sure that by discussing it I have lost any jewels that were in my future crown of motherhood glory. You can hear the jewels hitting the floor even now . . . *plink, plink, plink.*) My daughter is also a human being with a few (cough, cough, *control,* cough, cough) issues of her own. I love her more intensely than I can articulate, although she reminds me daily that my derriere is shaped like a heart, not the upside-down kind. She is right, but she still shouldn't bring it up.

I realize that many of the women who will read this book have experienced painful losses on either the Mother or the Daughter side. For those who are motherless daughters—due to death or abandonment or illness or someone else's choice, it is my prayer that you will be reminded of happier times and that it is still possible to be mothered by Other Mothers (see chapter 11). For those who are daughterless mothers, due to infertility or choice, or the untimely death of your daughter, I pray for healing in your heart and that you will find another "daughter of choice" who may desperately need your wisdom and love. It would be senseless to let all the love and nurture that God has placed inside you go to waste. Choose to love again. Be an Other Mother.

It is with trepidation that I dive headlong into this wonderful, messy subject. It is my desire that it is done with equal parts of love and laughter, as I believe that these are both vital ingredients in preserving the integrity and longevity of our mother/daughter relationship. If we lose our ability to love, then laughter is not possible. If we lose our ability to laugh at ourselves and with each other, then the love will seem duty bound and joyless.

Motherhood, mother-ness, mom. It's weird and completely unable to be fully decoded or fixed in this world. My goal is to help us all look at the whole Mom Thing with a little less drama and a lot more fun. So I hope, Gentle Reader, that you are ready to take a laughing look at your mom, yourself, and your kids with me as I do the same.

One important note: Do not highlight your personal favorite lines if you plan on passing this book along to your mom or your daughter. It could be incriminating.

no wonder they call it "labor"

O nce upon a time there were two people who decided to have a baby. One of these people was much more involved in the process than the other. The one who was more "heavily" involved (pun intended) would be The Mother. The one who watched it all happen, brought things to appease the varying moods and satisfy the bizarre cravings, and tied tennis shoes in the last trimester would be The Father. Men normally like to think of themselves as the strong, capable types. This is because they have never been through pregnancy, labor, and delivery.

It is a common male belief that they can somehow equate the passing of a kidney stone with childbirth. I have heard men say, "Aw, this is much worse than giving birth to a child." Having had a few kidney stones myself, I can attest that the pain is, indeed, excruciating. There are a few differences that must be noted, however:

- When the kidney stone is passed, it is normally caught in a strainer, not weighed in pounds and ounces, measured in inches, and given a name.

- When a kidney stone is passed, you do not get postpartum depression.
- Once a kidney stone exits your body, you are not responsible for 2 a.m. feedings, inoculations, disciplining it, or sending it to college.

I remember how much I wanted to have a baby when John and I first got married. It was foolish as we had no insurance and were both still in college at the time. But the combination of youthful optimism and total disregard for the amount of time or money this decision would cost us resulted in a pregnancy that started about the time we had been married five months. I was very excited and thought this was going to be the most blessed, beautiful time of my life.

That was, of course, until I had to go for my first prenatal visit.

Somewhere in my youthful optimism I failed to hear anything about the number of prenatal visits that were standard operating procedure or the details of this necessity. But let me say that they are an effective preparation for motherhood in general.

It starts with a weigh-in. These don't seem too bad the first couple of visits because the other person you are carrying inside of you is about the size of a pea. Peas don't weigh that much. So you are okay with the weigh-in. I can recall looking around at the eight- or nine-monthers sitting around the waiting room thinking, "I bet they weigh a ton! I'll *never* get that big." God was laughing at me just then, because peas grow. They become little peaches and then turn into cantaloupes and finally into watermelons. And thus the weigh-in becomes the most dreaded element of the visit.

I would dress in the lightest thing I could find by month seven, wear 2-ounce flip flops in the freezing weather, and ask to go to the bathroom twice before I went on the scale, but there was no denying the amount of butterbeans and Fudgesicles I was downing. The nurse would slide the metal weight on the balance beam farther to the right, farther to the right, farther to the right until you knew that you had reached the edge of I-Won't-Ever-Get-In-Those-Prepregnancy-Jeans-Again Zone. This will help prepare you for the upcoming humiliation that you will experience during delivery and every time your child decides to do something embarrassing in front of your in-laws.

Once they've elevated your blood pressure by giving you a number higher than you ever imagined for your weight, *then* they take your blood pressure. I don't know how they expect it to be normal when you have just come to the realization that you are really, really B-I-G, but if you use your Lamaze breathing techniques (more about that later), you can pant and blow yourself down to a medium-range systolic. This is the real reason that you should pay attention in Lamaze class.

Then they ask you to give a sample. Now, when I am discussing a "sample" at the obstetrics office, I am not talking about a trial-size cosmetic. What they are asking for is some of your . . . well . . . let's just call it "number one" for the sake of our more delicate readers. If you have never had to give a sample before, let me just tell you that it is not the easiest thing you'll do that day. Mainly because they want something called a "clean catch." It sounds like a term you would hear in circus-training-school-trapeze class ("Great job, Mr. Wallenda! That was a clean catch!"), but this entails precise stream/cup timing, which is difficult when your reach is hampered by the watermelon in your middle by month eight. Plus they give you the smallest size Dixie cup and expect you to get this done in an efficient manner. There are multiple problems here, one being that, if you did excuse yourself twice in preparation for the weigh-in, you are basically in a number one deficient status. There is no more being made right now as all available liquids are being marshaled in support of the person you are growing.

The second problem is that the term "clean catch" will never refer to your ability to get the sample without involving multiple antiseptic wipes and paper towels. I don't know if other people did this part better than me, but it always left me feeling like there must be a better technique than the one I was employing. All this must be intended to prepare you for the difficult body functions you will have to acquaint yourself with in order to deliver this child and keep it clean.

Next you will meet your obstetrical phlebotomist. These are usually women who have lurking latent sadistic tendencies and have been given the duty of filling a GINORMOUS vial of blood from your little veins to determine if this pregnancy is going swimmingly or if you need more vitamins. They tie off that little rubber tube at the top of your arm and look for a vein. I always looked away and tried to go to my happy place, but I found that there was no admittance to my happy place when there was a needle sticking in THE TENDEREST PART OF MY ARM. From these blood tests they can determine if you are iron deficient so that they can give you *even more* iron than is in your normal prenatal horse pill (aka "vitamin"), so that you can be *even more* constipated. They give you this much iron just in case you happen to be gestating an action hero.

Finally you make it to the exam room where you are put in a paper gown and asked to wait for the doctor to come and ask you the standard questions.

"How are you feeling today?" (In my mind, I would think, "*bigger,*" but I always answered, "oh, fine.")

"Any changes since your last visit? (In my mind, "*bigger,*" but I said, "not much.")

"Any problems you need to discuss with me?" (In my mind, "*besides how big I feel and how constipated I am from the extra iron tablets and how much I hate to have my blood drawn and how nauseated I am every morning from 6 to 11 a.m. and every time I smell meat cooking and how I can't remember how I used to look and how my ankles are all swollen and my husband must think I'm a cow and how much I doubt if I can actually be a very good mother . . .* sniff, sniff, blubber, blubber . . ." Out of my mouth, "no problems here, Doc!")

And every other month they have to do the full exam which involves scooting your lumbering middle down the table. This is not really a problem in the first two trimesters, but by the time you are at month seven there is a little more of you on the table than there used to be. This means that there is at least an inch of skin hanging over the edge of the paper exam table liner. When the doctor asks you to scoot down this skin often sticks to the vinyl of the table, making it impossible to scoot at all. This is another good reason to be kind to pregnant women.

The next phase of pregnancy is the Lamaze classes. I think these are more for the dads than the moms. Women *want* to know all about the birth process. We are the people buying and reading *What to Expect When You're Expecting.* We are Googling childbirth, talking to friends, stocking up on anecdotal tidbits in case our labor is like any of our friends' experiences. When we are at our own baby showers we are listening with rapt attention to all the horror stories about labor and delivery from our friends and family. It's like everyone tries to top each other in the misery category. This is why I believe friends and relatives should just get together and bring baby gifts, then let the pregnant mom-to-be come later.

But we are totally focused. We *want* to know. Men? Not so much. They are on a "need to know basis" only. And up until Lamaze they are just happier not knowing.

At Lamaze they make you watch films, which are something of a cross between films you see in biology class and the ones they make you watch in driver's ed — both fascinating and disturbing. I think it's the first time that most men get a clue as to what is about to happen to their woman and, frankly, they really did *not* want to know. But now they know. And now they must study to become great birthing partners.

This is a development of our century. For thousands of years women tended to other women during the labor and delivery of babies. Men waited outside and only came in afterward. For them childbirth was a womanly mystery, and they liked it like that. I believe that one day some women got together about this and agreed, "This is not right. If we've got to suffer like this to bring our offspring into the world, the least men can do is be there and watch us do this heroic thing." So they had to think up a job for the guy in all of this. And this was the best they could come up with: Feed us ice chips and chatter, "Breathe, honey. Focus, honey. Breathe, that's right, that was a good one. Good work, honey." As comedian Robin Williams puts it, "You have this myth that you're sharing the childbirth experience. Unless you're passing a bowling ball, I don't think so."

So Lamaze must be French for "give him something to do." And John *did* all the approved Lamaze phrases during the birth of our first child. In fact, there was a point where I told him that he might be OVERachieving in the talking area, and he was so nervous for me that he practically rubbed a hole in my hand. For the second one, he decided the talking part might be overrated and just patted my hand empathetically and got the nurse when I needed her. By the time we got to baby number three, he sat in the room, read the newspaper, and watched TV until it was time for me to push. But I was glad he was there for all three, if for no other reason than it made him a believer about the note from the doctor regarding limited "activities" for a while.

During labor, and it is appropriately named, by the way— there is a portion called "transition." This is when the baby is moving into the birth canal and stuff starts happening a little faster. In one Lamaze session they warn the men that the mom-to-be might become agitated during this phase and say things to him that are not very nice. This is to be expected and she doesn't really mean the awful things she is saying. I have come to believe that this phase is actually the culmination of all the aggravation of the prenatal visits backing up on her, and she feels the need to vent about it so she can rid herself of all that negativity before the baby comes into the world. That and the fact that she is totally *done* with this child being inside of her, and "transition" is the time during which she works up enough frustration to push it *out* of there.

Then she gets to become an amateur contortionist as the labor and delivery nurse asks her to put her knees up by her ears. Any other time in her life she would tell the nurse that she does *not* have the flexibility to achieve that in an unpregnated state, much less with this very large belly, but she is *so ready* to have this child that she will do any ridiculous thing she's told to do. In fact, if they told her that arising off the delivery table and turning a cartwheel and double back flip would have propelled that baby into the world, she probably would put Mary Lou Retton to shame. Instead, up go the knees and then she gets to push, and push, and push, and push.

"And push. And just one more push. That was a really good one. Let's have one more push. And another one. Good. Just one more." You try to block out the doctor and nurse and your husband "just one more-ing" you at least fifteen times, and finally: you get to see your baby. It's out! It's yours! It's crying! And the relief you feel at hearing that child cry is indescribable. Unfortunately, that is the *last* time you will feel relief to hear that wail. From now on you are responsible for attending to whatever need causes the child to make that sound. But for a moment you feel pure joy.

At least that's how childbirth happened for me. I know some women have Ceasarian sections, some have peaceful epidurals with a couple of pushes, and some adopt and skip the whole thing. But for me, getting three little Renfroes into the world was an effort of epic proportions. And that was just to get them up to sunlight.

I remember watching the Arnold Schwarzenegger movie *Junior* about men being able to gestate and thinking, "That would be great if they could just experience it once." And then I thought, "Nope. Then we would have zero population growth." So God knew which gender to make the birth-ers and which gender to make the ice chip dispensers.

After the baby has made its appearance into the world (and they don't really look like those Gerber ads for the first couple of days, but if you think of where they came from and how they got out, it's amazing they look as good as they do!) you get a cool little respite where they sleep a lot for about the same amount of time as your HMO will let you stay in the hospital. I don't know how the babies know how long that is, but they generally start waking up about the time you take them home. That is why new mothers cry.

Some of us also cry because we soon discover we've exchanged a belly with a mind of its own for breasts that now have their own little set of operating instructions, which are completely out of your control. I remember with my first baby I asked the nurse, "How will I know when my milk has come in?" She just nodded

and smiled and said, "Oh honey, you'll know." I kept thinking, "How? How will I know? This is my first . . . surely there's
some better answer than, 'You'll know.'" But she was right. On
the second day after I gave birth I was awakened to the vague
knowledge that there were Dolly Parton-worthy boulders sitting
where my normal breasts had been and they were as hard as boulders, too! This was a stunning development that certainly verified
the nurse's comment. I most definitely knew! I found it nothing
short of amazing that God had designed my body to come up with
enough milk to feed my newborn and (obviously) several others.
It was also great to have these gargantuan boulders to offset the
complete loss of waist. It almost balanced things out. But this was
also another signal that I was no longer in control. I think that was
the message of motherhood from the very first moment. "Anita,
you are no longer in control. Get used to it."

Responsibility without control: motherhood in a nutshell.

Any woman who has breast-fed can tell you that you are not
in control as your body develops something called your "let-down
reflex." This is why lactating females must have some sort of shield
or padding in their bras at all times. For the first week or so I used
the shields that they tell you are made for your lactating needs.
They're round, they're soft, they cost money, and they have to be
washed. Plus they also hold less than an ounce of milk before they
start leaking. Now I was what you might call a "lactating machine."
Call me "Elsie the Contented Cow." I produced an ounce in the
first nanosecond that my milk let down. Fortunately I discovered
Viva paper towels (soft, strong, absorbent, affordable, disposable!).

If you fold two of them into quarters you can absorb half the Ohio River if need be. These squares folded and inserted into your bra look really silly under normal clothing, but at this time of your life you are no longer wearing normal clothing. You are not wearing maternity, but you're not yet able to fit into anything prepregnancy. This is when your husband's shirts (which unbutton nicely for breast-feeding) and hospital scrub pants fill the bill nicely.

I can recall being in the grocery store without my child (who was sleeping at home with Dad) and hearing someone else's baby cry over on aisle 7. It did not matter that this was not my child. This was A Child That I Was Capable of Feeding. My brain told my breasts that this was a DefCom 4 situation and, even before I could try to divert my mind with other thoughts (What are the state capitals? What is my mother's social security number? What is the square root of pi?), I began to soak my trusty Viva. I guess I didn't realize that if you are breastfeeding you become The Original Meals on Heels. It is actually a good thing because, at least eight or ten times a day you get to excuse yourself from the rest of the world and take a little time with just you and your baby. It did take extra time and sometimes it wasn't all that convenient, but I was just too lazy to wash all those bottles.

I believe that the beginnings of this ride called motherhood are designed to let you know that you are in for some hard work, some tough situations, a loss of control, and a new space for adventure and joy in your life. It's the hardest job you'll ever love.

a little mayo
with the
momwich

There are certain things you start to say when you reach a certain age (like, "What is with all that noise on the radio?" and "Young people used to have manners in this country."). You can actually track how close you are to getting put in a nursing home by the frequency of these sorts of phrases in your daily conversations.

So, at the risk of sounding elderly, weren't the TV commercials better back in the sixties and seventies? Other than the really bad polyester outfits, the products were all designed to make our lives better and to shave the time we spent preparing meals. We had Tang—the orange flavored drink that the astronauts drank! We watched commercials for Hungry Man TV dinners, and you had your choice of mixing biscuits (Bisquick) or popping them out of a can (Pillsbury).

One of the more interesting (genderwise, that is) food commercials was one that implied a real *manly* man would never eat a regular sloppy joe *sand*wich, he needed a "Manwich" (think Tim "The Toolman" Taylor making his grunting noises). Wouldn't you think that all the bra-burning militant feminists of that era would have protested this stereotypical product labeling by boycotting Manwich? Not on your life! I have no idea what testosterone-driven ad agent thought that name would sell more sauce, but he must've been a genius because it's still on the grocery store shelves to this day.

I have experienced something slightly different than a Manwich. I have been both a bread slice and I have been the filling in what I call a "Momwich." This is a scenario where three generations of women (mother and a daughter and her daughter) all live under one roof. Sometimes it's by choice, sometimes it's of necessity, but it's always an interesting mix.

When I was two years old, my biological father left my mother and me. It was devastating for my mom, and she would have been unable to support us both had we not moved in with her parents. My mom has told me that, as my grandfather was a man given to fits of rage, she was reluctant to move back home but really had no choice financially. So it was that from the age of two until I was ten, I was the younger piece of bread in a Momwich. I have asked my mom what it was like for her to move back in with her mother at that time in her life, and she said it was a comfort to have her mom there daily during the time when she was healing from the emotional wounds of divorce and that her mother, ever the strong soul and optimist, acted as a buffer between her and her father.

My earliest childhood memories include spending lots of time with my Nana (because my mom was working) and playing out on the farm. The days were slow, just as they should be when you are a child and have no reason to feel the passage of time. I recall feeling quite loved by my Nana and my mom (also by my grand-father, who in his older years was more docile), so this Momwich was a blessing for me and provided stability in my early life. It also gave my mom a few years of emotional haven where she could find her confidence again. My grandmother believed that God would send my mom a soulmate (since the dating pool in our little town was pret-ty small!), and mom was resolute to hold out for someone who would love her deeply. When John Pulliam moved to Burnet to work at a fish hatchery, Mom and John fell in love and married, so the Momwich was no longer necessary. Interestingly enough, Nana would continue to spend parts of the year with us even when we moved from Texas to Virginia. Momwiches are enduring.

And I've found that Momwiches can morph over time, as I am now the middle part of one. I am the meaty sauce, the daughter/mother in between my mom and my daughter, and the joe can get pretty sloppy some days. When we moved to Atlanta several years ago, my parents were already in the area living on the opposite side of town. My dad's job took him on overseas trips frequently, so when Dad was out of the country Mom would stay with us so that she wouldn't have to be alone. At the same time I was start-ing to travel more frequently for my own work and ministry, and Mom and Dad would come over on those weekends to help out with the kids.

After a few months it occurred to us that we could save a boat-load of money if we combined our incomes and bought a single house large enough for all of us. It would solve lots of problems with one fell swoop. So we found a place with three floors (so we could all ding the bell and retreat to our separate areas should the closeness start to feel—well . . . too close).

When people would hear of our arrangement they would sort of drop their jaw in amazement and ask, "How does that ever work?" And we would explain that we were all pretty busy people and hardly ever home all at the same time and we just *made* it work. My dad and my husband were great friends and all the guys would do guy things, and my mom took over the laundry room (no problem with that here!), and we just sort of agreed on what rooms got decorated by whom. Mostly no problems.

Until my mom's life changed forever.

My dad was Mom's haven, her place to vent and work things through emotionally. Tragically, about a year and a half after we moved in together, my dad died of pancreatic cancer. My mom's top part of the Momwich was scorched by grief. Within a few months of my dad's death she had surgery on her Achilles tendon and was hobbled for months. I thought it was ironic that her body mimicked her emotional state—it was like she was having to learn to walk all over again at the same time she was having to learn how to live all over again.

No longer being a wife after twenty-five years of happy marriage, Mom's core identity was suddenly undercut. I guess I shouldn't have been surprised when, in scrambling to find a sense of herself and a meaningful role in our revised family dynamic, she latched on to her intermittent Momhood with new and vigorous . . . umm . . . enthusiasm. This time around, however, she was leapfrogging a generation and aiming straight at trying to get *my* kids to toe *her* line. She had some legitimate issues about them not *always* respecting her and not *always* being as helpful as they could be, but my thoughts were, "What kids are always 100 percent in either of those areas? And what if I kinda agree with them that your standards of cleanliness might be a little high?"

Since there were some definite differences between how I was choosing to parent my kids and how I was raised, the whole issue of parenting became a huge source of contention for us for a couple of years. My mom saw some of my parenting decisions as invalidating my upbringing or not respecting the way she wanted things done, but I had definite ideas of what I thought was essential. Basically, our lists did not match, and this created a lot of tension.

My mom will be the first to admit that part of the problem was that she had raised only me. An "only." She had never dealt with multiples nor boys, so she believed everything should be as orderly and easy with three as it was with one. I, personally, enjoy chaos — at least in small doses. We no longer have as many of those issues as the boys have grown up and moved away (for most of the year). The rest of us don't make quite as big of a mess.

On the other side of my Momwich is my daughter, Elyse. She's now in her teens and can remember only a little bit of life before the Momwich. I know that her experience in this scenario is different than mine was simply because of three things: (1) She became the underlying layer later in her life (she was eight when we started the present Momwich), (2) She had older brothers in it with her, and

(3) She's a different temperament than I am. Elyse is an observer and a pretty good one to get the gist of situations without much explanation. She has a high Emotional Intelligence Quotient, and she has always been her own girl.

Although she was born into a family with two older brothers, Elyse has always had a strong sense of her femininity and a firm resolve to not put up with much nonsense. She will not suffer boredom long (she regularly walks out on movies that are predictable). She knows what she likes and what doesn't fit her taste anymore. It is almost a family joke that on any given day she will just decide she doesn't like something and she will set it out into the hall, like "whenever the hall fairy comes around, she will need to pick this up and remove it from my presence." This sends her pack rat, sentimental dad into fits. He will shake his head and say, "Elyse! How could you get rid of this?" Of course, to him, everything is "special."

I know it is sometimes difficult for Elyse to be mothered by two generations at the same time. Some things are straight-up generational issues — like clothes and music tastes — and we fall out along the lines of our eras. Some differences are in our needs for boundaries (Elyse needs a *lot*, I need some, Mom doesn't need any or recognize them unless you put up an electric fence). Some days I do feel the squish of the Momwich. Mom will (at times) intimate that I'm not quite getting the Mom job done with Elyse in a certain area, and Elyse will be asking me to tell Mom to make herself a little more scarce when her friends come over, and *these* are the moments you wish, for a little while, that you only had one side of the bun or the other. But I love both the buns—and, besides, an open face sandwich isn't on the menu right now.

But because my daughter has a strong sense of her uniqueness, I think the Momwich actually helps her to hold on to herself in a house with two other strong women. I don't think Elyse and my mom have the same sort of relationship they might have if they had the normal amount of space that grandmothers and granddaughters have between them. I don't know if that is something they might miss with each other. But there is something to be said for being a part of the every day. And I wonder how it will turn out over time. We've been in our current Momwich configuration for almost a decade and we are all growing and morphing and changing and trying to remain loving through it all. Mom is moving some of her time and interests out of the house, and Elyse is perched on the edge of the nest. It's not that hard to imagine that I could be the top bun in another kind of Momwich someday.

I also wonder how many women find themselves, at different times in their lives, in a Momwich. It certainly isn't something you dream about as a child. I don't think anyone, when she is seven years old and dreaming about her adult life says, "Man, I can't wait to grow up so I can keep living with my mother!" But life brings to us situations that change our idea of "normal" and give us a chance to see whether the faith and grace we profess to possess is all talky, talky and no walky, walky. And it gives a daily proving ground for love to triumph through dysfunction.

I've found that Momwiches are a lot like Manwiches: meaty,

messy, alternately sloppy and satisfying. Like the Manwich, a Momwich is a slightly heavier emotional portion than many would even attempt to bite off, but we are all three the stronger women for it.

stretch
marks

Y ou might be a mom if . . .

   . . . you've had a permanent "tired feeling between your
     eyes" for several years in a row.

   . . . you think nothing of eating food off other people's
     plates.

   . . . you automatically grab thirty napkins from the
     dispenser at any fast food restaurant even if you are
     dining alone.

   . . . you have exact change for lunch money stashed in
     secret places for emergencies, even though you have
     no elementary school children left at home.

   . . . you've ever carried a lost tooth around in a tissue in
     your purse in order to stash it under a pillow, replace
     it with tooth fairy money, and then transfer it to your
     jewelry box.

   . . . you can accurately reel off each of your children's

snack preferences and food allergies while under
general anesthesia.

. . . you have Wet Wipes and paper towels strategically
stashed in every car and purse that you own.

. . . you automatically flail your arm when you make a
sudden stop in an attempt to be the air bag for your
children — even though it's been ten years since you
were hauling them around on a regular basis.

. . . you refuse to swim in public because you have stretch
marks to beat the band.

Skin is the largest organ of the human body. It's also a road-
map of all you've been through in your life. Every line and crease
on your body is the result of time and repetitive movement. In the
neck of suburbia where we make our home there are "medi-spas"
popping up like Starbucks. They are like regular day spas with
the exception that they are medically supervised, and the people
who work there are certified to inject you with stuff. I'm not fond
enough of needles to do my own research, but I have heard that
you can go and have a nonsurgical lift over lunch and get rid of
the little lines around your eyes and mouth in about the same
amount of time it takes to get a pedicure. You can also get shot
up with Restilayne or Botox to fill and paralyze your creases, but
it freezes your face to the point that your friends will not be able
to "read" any expressions and you may consequently end up with
more personal problems than your beauty can fix.

It has always been my personal aim to have the best laugh lines

in my neighborhood. If you laugh a lot it will show. I'm kinda looking forward to that. But I have also reached a time in my life when
it's not unusual for me to get completely freaked out by just looking down at my hand on the steering wheel of the car. Sometimes
I see it there like it isn't really attached to me. I see the crepey skin
that looks so thin and a couple of age spots and think, "*Whose hand
is that?*" like it isn't mine. I also have this strange detached curios-
ity when I see how my eye skin isn't bouncing back when I use my
pencil eyeliner. It's like the skin scrunches up as the pencil moves
it to one side—and then it just stays there! What is up with that?
It used to spring back into place immediately; but now, if I don't
nudge it back it's like it forgot where to go. Some days it makes
me laugh and other days I just don't know how to handle it. More
moisturizer, liquid eyeliner, more acceptance of my own skin.

It's easy to spot the moms who are away from their kids on a
beach or a cruise. The first clue is the way they whip their head
around when someone else's kid yells, "Mom!"—like it's an
uncontrollable Pavlovian response. The other dead giveaway is the
pareo they use to cover up their stretch marks. Now I know that
women can have them for other reasons, but most women tend to
get them from carrying a child. It's the rapid weight gain-weight
loss that causes these funky stripes to set in and, as easy as they are
to come on, they are almost impossible to get off.

There is now a whole industry devoted to helping us erase this
Badge of Motherhood from our stomachs and thighs. They promise to moisturize, tone, jiggle, and chemically reduce the size of our
stretch marks. They will take our money and our time, but none

of them promise to *actually get rid of* the stripes. Once you've got 'em, you've got 'em. Some women contend that they did not get them in the first place because they moisturized excessively during pregnancy. I don't know who these women are, but they must not have been pregnant in the south in the summer. I cannot imagine moisturizing for the prevention of stretch marks when the cocoa or shay butter would have made my huge pregnancy granny panties stick to the humid, icky-hot, summertime-in-Mississippi belly any more than they already were. Willingly I would have stretch marks instead of feeling like a basting Butterball in the sweltering southern heat.

So I have them. They are the proof that God made my skin with enough elastic to accommodate the carrying of children. And they're actually pretty ingenious when you think of the alternative. If our skin wasn't made to stretch and then return (almost) to its former shape, it would either have to tear or get bigger and just stay that way. Neither seems like a good way to go.

But most of the stretch marks that women carry with them are the ones you can't see as easily. Not because they never don a swimsuit, but because a great many of the stretch marks we acquire are internal. These Emotional Stretch Marks are the ones that mothers and daughters acquire from each other. As stretching is always the prerequisite to growth it can feel tight and uncomfortable (ask any kid in a growth spurt), and mothers and daughters have an intimate, intuitive way of knowing when it's time for a choice between growth or stagnation—and that growth requires a stretch, even if it hurts a little.

You might hear people say, when someone gets injured, "Wow, that's gonna leave a mark." By this they are referring to some sort of permanent reminder of that incident. I believe that every mother has the ability to mark her daughter for better or worse. In the way that we all have belly buttons, we are all marked forever by our mothers. Some have mothers that mark them in powerfully loving ways, tenderly caring for them and helping them mature into the women God designed them to be, blessing them to pursue their God-given abilities and destiny, releasing them from their nurture into their own future. Others have mothers who have marked them in hurtful ways, refusing to love them unconditionally, rejecting them while clinging to them and insisting that they live out their mother's unfulfilled dreams, denying their distinct, admirable gifts. These marks are lasting, too. Sometimes they take years to heal. In time they may fade, but they are never completely gone.

When we are young girls it is part of the gift of a mother to stretch us. Our moms may put us in less-than-comfortable situations that help us see that we can do more than we think we can and that we are capable of handling things beyond our comfort zones. When Elyse was about eight years old she was with me on a trip to a women's conference in another state. The meeting was in a hotel conference center and she had been helping me with the product table when we ran out of change. Elyse came to me to inform me of the impending emergency but it was almost time for the next session to start so I told her to take two $20 bills, go down to the restaurant (about twenty yards down the hall), and exchange them for fives. She looked at me like I'd just told her to jump in a spacecraft and fly to the moon.

"Mom, I don't know anyone in that restaurant! I can't do that!"

"Yes, you can."

For a timid eight-year-old, having to walk down that hall and ask for something she needed from a stranger was a stretching experience. Not only did she accomplish it but she hasn't had much trouble asking for most anything she needs since.

As a daughter and the mother of a daughter, I have come to see that daughters can also leave Emotional Stretch Marks on their mothers. Most of us have witnessed this on a superficial level when a daughter will tell her mom that her stale hairdo has got to go, or that her mom could use some updating in the wardrobe department. Usually Mom will accept this kind of thing from her daughter because she knows that it's said partly out of love. Elyse will let me know when I am losing touch with what is current and, though we don't share the same taste in clothes, I will take her opinion into consideration. What moms won't change for love they will consider changing to save their child humiliation.

But when the areas that are being stretched move to more tender parts of us the immediate response won't always be, "Hey, great! I'm ready to stretch a little. Bring it on!" More often the challenge is met with some resistance and a questioning of motives. Stretching can be initially uncomfortable and just plain hard.

The two years following my father's death were very difficult for my mom as she struggled with how to begin to make a life without this man whom she had loved for so long. I imagine that for women who have had a cold or uncaring husband that transition may not be so hard, but my dad loved my mom so beautifully and completely that it became almost impossible for her to imagine any lasting happiness without him. She was adrift for a while, as if she had lost all her moorings. She was angry with God for allowing her soul mate to suffer and leave her. She didn't feel comfortable socializing with the same friends that they had been friends with as couples (it made her miss Dad so much more). She didn't want to go to the same church (too many memories) and didn't have a job outside the home. It was like someone had taken my mom's world and left it in the dryer too long—it shrunk.

Sometimes this was hard for us, because John and I and Mom's three grandchildren became her whole world. It was hard for me to know where the lines were regarding "honoring" her, being sympathetic toward her, allowing her time to heal, and enabling her to continue to let the size of her world shrink. Her feelings were very close to the surface and fragile, so if we didn't say something just right or respond in a certain way, she would cry at the drop of a hat. It wasn't because what we said was necessarily wrong or disrespectful, it's just that when your world includes only a few people you cannot possibly get all of your validation from them. It's simply not realistic.

At the end of the second year as my mom was starting to feel that she might actually make it, we were wrapping up a few days with some girlfriends at the beach. As she and I sat in the airport, waiting to go back home, she could tell that I was unusually quiet. I don't recall her doing anything particularly aggravating, but it just seemed like she was always *there*—wherever I was. I was in dire need of some space. When she asked what was wrong with me I blurted out, "Mom, you've got to get your own life!" She asked me what I meant by that, and I told her that I couldn't make that determination for her, but she had to start exploring it.

She was more than a little stunned and, frankly, hurt. I don't think I meant to be hurtful, but I had been walking on emotional eggshells ever since Dad died, and I felt that the time for subtle hints had long since passed. So when we got home, she cried about it and immediately made plans to go to Texas to spend some time with her sisters and try to figure out what "her own life" might entail. I felt that she had overreacted to what I said, but any action that she was taking—even rash, reactive action—was somehow empowering to her and was "stretching" her beyond what she had been able to do to this point. She did, in fact, go to Texas to explore other options in where and how she would live and decided that making a move out west was not the best thing for her to do. But out of that trip she was able to make some conscious decisions about her life that she might not have made (or made much later) had I not said something uncomfortable, stretching.

I am happy to say that Mom's world is significantly larger now. She works part time and loves, loves, LOVES helping people. She really is one of the friendliest people you will ever meet. We call her "The Unofficial Biographer" because she will have people telling details about their life in two minutes flat. And the funny thing is, she will tell *us* all about a person—". . . and she's got a twenty-two-year-old daughter in medical school in Boston and they have a horse farm and this woman has lived all over the country and she used to be a model for a hand cream company . . ."—and we'll say, "Mom, what was her name?" And Mom will say, "Oh, I don't remember." We fall out laughing. Who needs a name when you have all the other details?

In the six years since Dad passed, Mom (who has always had a strong soprano voice) had not been able to rejoin the world of music, but she has recently found her place in the choir at church and is enjoying singing once again. It is good to see her find her "song" again. And when the Beach Girls get together, I no longer have the urge to tell her to "get a life," as she is expanding her circle with all sorts of new people to Unofficially Biographize.

There are times when Stretch Marks are called for in our Mother/Daughter relationships. We can say things to each other that no other human on the face of the earth can say. And, yes, sometimes it may sting a little. But it might be The Thing we needed to hear at that moment to motivate us to reach higher and to go further than we have had the will to stretch before. The tricky part is to figure out how to Stretch but not Snap. If we push too hard we have left the area of love and concern and reached into a dangerous zone of cruelty or retaliation. Wherever the aim is stretching, truth will be spoken with love and the desire will be for the good of the person without permanently widening the chasm between us.

As mothers and daughters we have the privilege to hold each others' hands with empathy and compassion and to give each other a timely kick to the derriere when we see that motivation is the need of the hour. Both are necessary to keep our hearts moving forward and growing toward the God-breathed destiny that we are called to fulfill in this life.

These are the Stretch Marks made of love.

baby books and other blueprints

Remember back when people were all about getting into therapy? Having their very own therapist? Letting go of their inner angst, getting in touch with their inner child? This was a development of the late 1950s that blossomed in the 1960s and eventually became The Thing To Do. Even if you didn't have serious issues you weren't really hip unless you could drop the words "My therapist says . . ." into everyday conversation. It was almost a status symbol. If you had enough money you could pay for someone to attentively listen to your problems. The less affluent had to settle for talking to each other. For free.

It seems that therapy territory usually includes going way back and delving into complicated issues like the way you were potty trained or if you never had a pony, and professional therapists use this information to figure out why you are having trouble moving forward with your life. This method insists that you are probably "stuck" somewhere in your past, and if you could just get unstuck all would be right with the world. This is partly true, but maybe you are stuck there because deep down you really liked 1982. Why else would you have a modified mullet, parachute pants in your closet, and the boxed set of "The Bangles Greatest Hits"?

This business of therapy became specialized over the years and eventually you could choose from private therapy sessions (expensive but you get the therapist's complete attention—unless she's pretending to be listening while making out her grocery list), group therapy (where you can share your innermost thoughts with complete strangers who pretend not to judge you but are sitting there collecting evidence to prove that they aren't the craziest one in the group), shock therapy (do not try this at home), pet therapy (Fido will love you, dogs love everyone), regression therapy (premise: if they take you back to the origin of the mullet you can let go of it and embrace a blunt cut), and primal scream therapy (which originated in the Labor and Delivery Room, by the way).

I really can't comment on the best approach as I've never been in any long-term therapy—though some might believe I need it. But I know that it has helped many people find some level of personal clarity and healing and that it has enriched many therapists. Some people extol its virtues, others think it's a waste of time and money. I personally swear by massage therapy, chocolate therapy, and retail therapy (preferably a combination of all three in the same afternoon).

It seems to me that our culture has made a therapeutic shift in recent years. People don't really have hunks of time to spend sifting through their past for clues to their current issues. We are now enlightened enough to know that all that digging around in the past could just drag us down and run up our bills. Besides, we are people with places to go, people to see, things to do! We are all hopped up on espresso and running at such a frantic pace that an hour of therapy would almost be indulgent, impossible. No time!

Enter the latest and hippest Non-Therapy Therapy called "Life Coaching." Life Coaches don't care how you were potty trained or what traumatic things happened to you in junior high school. Well, it's not really that they *don't care*, it's more that the past is not their area of expertise. They just want to know where you want to go from here and what is stopping you. There are certification programs for Life Coaches and professional associations of Life Coaches. I'll bet there are even seminars for Life Coaches where they coach each other. These Life Coaches ask prodding questions in an effort to get you to articulate your dreams. Then they give you a weekly dose of encouragement. ("You can do it! Let's write down some actions steps!") They call you at an appointed time each week to pester you until you do the thing you said you needed to do JUST SO THEY WILL LEAVE YOU ALONE. They will hold your hand *and* kick your posterior.

I believe that back in the day this used to be called mothering. Moms were the Original Life Coaches. And moms really can't help it. From the time we know that we are going to have a baby we are filled with wonderment. We wonder if it's going to be a boy or a girl. We wonder if the baby is going to be all right physically and mentally. We wonder if the music we are listening to is going to make the child smarter or if the last meal we ate is going to turn the baby against sweet potatoes. This tendency to wonder can keep us awake at night and drive us to distraction.

Perhaps the main thing moms wonder about is what their kids are going to be when they grow up. Not only do we wonder, we plan. Oh, we never admit to it (okay, so Jewish mothers do) but most of us do plan our children's lives in our heads. We know that God loves you and has a wonderful plan for your life, and we're pretty sure that He has imparted that insight directly to us.

Moms can "guide" you early in your interests because they are the ones who initiate most of your activities when you are a kid. Moms control the calendar + moms have wheels + moms have the power of withholding your allowance = you must participate in whatever they sign you up for. Does it matter that you have absolutely no interest in being a ballerina? No. Mom says ballet lessons will help you with your balance and coordination. Does Mom care if you like T-ball or not? Nope, the experience will help you play well with others. Do you have any aptitude for gymnastics? Piano? No matter. Even if you're the lamest tumbler on the mat your mom may envision you at the qualifying round for the Olympics just a few years from now. If you are a klutz on the keyboard she still sees you taking a bow at Carnegie Hall.

If you take a look at your baby book, you can find out many things about how your mom envisioned your future. These record books hold many clues about your mom's earliest blueprint for her little angel. How were you dressed for those first pictures? Some moms put their little girls in all sorts of frou-frou lacy itchy stuff and then wonder why the baby cries throughout the photo session. Maybe your mom dressed you in princess attire or in a cowgirl outfit. You can probably just take either of those literally. Maybe you weren't dressed at all . . . and what might THAT mean? Surely such a find warrants a session or two of therapy. But moms do love those nudie baby photos. Plus, all moms secretly enjoy carrying a little blackmail potential in their hip pocket.

Of course what you might find in your baby book also depends on your birth order. You can tell which child a baby book belongs to just by looking at it. Firstborns — lots and lots of photos, photos of you inhaling and exhaling, photos of you sleeping and waking, photos of every milestone, locks of hair from your first haircut, every date of your immunizations, verbatim transcripts of what the pediatrician said at your checkup, etc. Second children — exactly half the photos but none of the extras. Third child? You're lucky if you even *have* a baby book, and you should feel greatly loved and treasured if your mom got your birth certificate stuck in there! For children whose birth order is third or higher, your mom had possibly run out of ideas for her kids' futures by then and was just concentrating on keeping everyone alive. This is why children farther down the birth order must have a lot of determination and self-motivation. The Mom Life Coach was worn down before she got to you.

Other adults are happy to help you find your way in life, too. Aunts and grandmas are constantly asking children, "So what do you want to be when you grow up?" If you can't come up with an acceptable answer in a matter of seconds they will look at your mom with their brows all furrowed as if to intimate that she hasn't taken you to quite enough after-school activities. I love the fact that kids never choose a boring career early in their lives. They are going to be something exciting! No kid ever says, "I want to be an accountant" or, "When I grow up I want to be one of those telephone customer service reps." Nope—it's always some really exhilarating job like tightrope walker or veterinarian or doctor or policeman.

Why *do* adults ask little kids what they want to be when they grow up? Comedian Paula Poundstone says that we are constantly asking kids that question because we are still looking for hints for ourselves. I think adults are trying to make sure that your plans in life are aimed at something that doesn't involve criminal intent lest they need to take immediate diversionary tactics. Either way, I think it's wrong to make kids think about choosing a career that early. How can they know what they might do for a living twenty-five years down the road? I don't think I knew what I really loved to do until I was in my mid-thirties, and I'm still discovering different bunny trails every year. We find out what we are supposed to be doing by a long process of trial and error that usually ends up with us doing what we were supposed to be doing all along, but we couldn't have arrived at that conclusion based on whatever we told our aunt when we were seven years old.

As a child you can also pick up vibes about your mom's blueprint for you by what she says about *other* people's choices. "Did you hear about that Abbott girl down the street? I ran into her mother's sister down at the car wash and she told me that girl is planning on going to veterinary school for eight years! Goodness, I can't believe she would choose a profession where you have to go to school for that long—she'll practically be an old maid by the time she finishes—and then deal with animal illnesses day in and day out and day in and day out . . ." This is a stealthy way for her to discuss her opinions about your potential issues without actually discussing *you*. But you always know that the point was for your benefit.

The Life Coach Mom swings into high gear during her child's senior high school years. This is when she will collect pamphlets for the college closest to home and conveniently leave them lying around on the floor of your bathroom or taped to the steering wheel of your car. Subtle, we are not.

As Elyse is sliding into her last year of high school, it is everything I can do not to tell her The Plan. Oh, I've got one, all right. It's brilliant. But I also know that my daughter is at the age where I have to use buckets of reverse psychology. If there's anything I really want her to do I have found it best to forbid it. So I am forbidding all sorts of things, like attending a local college. Absolutely not! And living at home the first couple of years? Out of the question! I'm telling her to marry early—very early! Of course, as soon as she reads this chapter the jig will be up.

It is both the best and worst day of a mom's life when she drops Junior or Juniorette off at college or sees them enter the military or sends them off on their new life adventure. Then we spend our time wondering if we equipped them well or if our babies will make great choices with their lives. Kids wonder when we will ever recognize their maturity and stop giving them "input," but I tell you that years and years of Life Coaching cannot be undone all at once. Elyse thinks I turn everything into a lecture, but if she only knew how much I was *editing* she would hand me a trophy.

Little by little moms learn not to say EVERYTHING we are thinking ALL the time. Sometimes we use the reverse psychology method. Sometimes we bite our tongues 'til they bleed. But that doesn't mean we aren't still thinking it.

eat this,
you'll
feel better

God bless General Mills for inventing Cheerios, and God bless Dow Chemical for inventing Ziploc baggies. Between the two of them the world is a happier place.

I can't imagine what moms did before there were Cheerios. What food item served as the multipurpose snack before we had those cute little o's that are just right for Baby's little fingers to practice her manual dexterity as she picks one up and gets it into her mouth? A half a Ziploc of Cheerios has gotten many moms through airplane trips, long rides to Grandma's house, and various other situations where all you need is to buy yourself a little time between the last meal you fed the child and the next meal you can feed the child. If you are smart you will carry a bag of these in your carry-on luggage on a plane (even if you haven't had a two-year-old for twenty years) because you never know if the mom who sits next to you with a toddler may have gone through her last bag of Cheerios in the gate area, and it could be a really long plane ride without them.

Because that's what moms do: children cry, moms feed.

There's an old joke that goes, "What's the difference between an Italian mother, a Jewish mother, a Japanese mother, and an Irish mother?"

"The accent."

And the spice they add to the comfort food.

It's universal, it's cross-cultural, it's our primal connection with our child. It is Job #1 upon becoming a mom and our Normal Default Mode when we find ourselves fresh out of ideas. We feed when the children are happy, feed when they're sad, feed when they're confused. It doesn't matter what the impetus is. Whether we need to celebrate, drown our sorrows, or have a moment of connection that involves carbohydrates, the response is the same: "Here. Eat this. You'll feel better."

In the movie *My Big Fat Greek Wedding*, the mom is a Classic Feeder.

Maria Portokalos: "Ian, are you hungry?"

Ian Miller: "Uh no, I already ate."

Maria Portokalos: "Okay, I make you something."

Traditional mothers want to fatten you up. You have never heard anyone compliment a new mother by saying, "Look — your baby seems to have about 2 percent body fat. This is way below the national average and will make for a muscular child. Great job!" No. We want to see a baby that has chubby little cheeks, a couple of chins and double knees. In some strange way it warms our hearts to know that this baby could survive a season of food scarcity (like maybe going an hour without the Cheerios). This must be some leftover response to the days when there were actual lean times during which you needed some stored up fat to survive. We don't exactly have a recent history of "lean times" in the United States. We have eighteen hour a day access to Pizza Hut/Taco Bell/Wendy's/Krispy Kreme.

I don't know if we'll ever get away from the "fat baby = healthy baby" idea, but regardless, moms just want their children to eat. We worry if you don't eat. We worry if you don't eat enough. We worry that you don't eat the right things. For moms, food is the emotional temperature gauge. If you aren't eating, something must be wrong, and if you are eating, all must be okay. We are emotionally sturdy and can withstand a lot, but if you want your mom in the loony bin, just start rejecting food. We can't take it.

Even moms who consider themselves seriously deficient in the kitchen (I call them "4 Alarm Cooks"—whenever they try to cook four smoke alarms go off) have their own little specialties that are their secret calling card for the children. Everybody has *something* that they make better than anyone else—even if it's just triple-decker s'mores, grilled cheese sandwiches with two kinds of cheese melted just right and crispy bread, extra tangy Kool-Aid, crustless PBJ's with Skippy. No real skill involved here, just the Special Mom Touch.

My Nana used to make me cheese toast in the regular oven. When it got just hot enough the whole slice of cheese would get a big bubble underneath it and Nana would burn the edges just a tad to make them extra crisp. She also made the most amazing garlic dill pickles from the cucumbers and dill of her very own garden. My mom has a way with roast beef, green beans, and rolls. There is nothing quite like opening the front door of the house and having that smell of a roast in the oven and fluffy yeast rolls (and the gravy . . .) hit you square in the nostrils. It announces, "Come in! Park your feet under the table and ingest my love!" And all my kids have their special requests—Calvin loves stroganoff, Austin likes a pot of chili so he can make Frito Chili Pie, and the whole family knows that absolutely *nobody* trumps my strawberry shortcake. If Elyse is needing a little food therapy I stir up some of my Chocolate Gravy and pop some Pillsbury Crescent Rolls in the oven. If you swim one of those flaky rolls in a bowl of chocolate gravy (yes, chocolate + gravy will cure anything), broken hearts can mend, hurtful words can fade, PMS can subside, and the world is guaranteed to be set aright upon its axis.

Moms just *know things* about food. They know that the creamy, cheesy goo of a dish of macaroni and cheese can put some distance between their child and a bad day. We even know that food can be medicinal. Take chicken soup, for example. Moms have known for years that it does something to fight off infection, open the sinuses, and make you feel better. Medical science is now backing that by verifying that something in the chicken soup actually fights inflammation and strengthens the immune system. The scientists can't say for sure what the magic ingredient *is*, they just know it's doing the job. The question is, how did moms know before the scientists? Soon scientists will be able to corroborate that you actually *do* get colds from going outside with a wet head or that faces *do* freeze like that.

It is worth pondering—how did we arrive at our decisions to eat certain foods? (if you ever ponder such things). Through the centuries, who decided which foods deserved a place on the grocery shelf and which ones just didn't cut it? It makes you wonder what the trial and error process might have been. I mean, I wonder how many people had to die mysteriously and suddenly before they figured out that certain mushrooms and berries were poisonous. And who was the first person to say, "Oh look! There is a white orb coming forth from that chicken's posterior. Let's hard boil it, fry it, scramble it, omelette it, benedict it, and crepe it." Or who was the one who decided that the stuff that the calves were drinking would be a fine addition to our diet? (For all you milk lovers out there, I just want to point out that we are the only mammals that drink milk after we are infants AND it's the milk of another species. *Eeeewwwwww.*) In the early days of civilization I'm sure that moms got a boatload of guilt from serving things to their kids that killed them. In those days being a picky eater might have been a survival advantage, especially if you didn't really like mushrooms or berries anyway. This may be why contemporary moms announce a little extra loudly, "Eat it. It won't kill you." Because we may have some latent residual guilt over foods that actually *did* kill centuries ago.

With our daughters the whole "Are you eating? Why aren't you eating? How much are you eating?" thing can be an emotional minefield. You don't have to be a clinical psychologist to witness the growing number of women (young and old alike) with eating disorders. The prevailing wisdom is that it has little to do with how a woman looks but everything to do with how she feels about how she looks and her desire to exercise control over her life. This obsession is fueled by a society driven to extremes in fashion, sometimes in the name of "fitness."

I pray for the day when our society values health more than looks and inner wholeness and beauty more than how the jeans fit. In the Sermon on the Mount Jesus made it clear that the food/clothes issue only underscores our value to God. Jesus inextricably linked the two things when he said, "If you decide for God, living a life of God-worship, it follows that you don't fuss about what's on the table at mealtimes or whether the clothes in your closet are in fashion. There is far more to your life than the food you put in your stomach, more to your outer appearance than the clothes you hang on your body. Look at the birds, free and unfettered, not tied down to a job description, careless in the care of God. And you count far more to him than birds" (Matthew 6:25-26).

It seems that when we become consumed with spirit life, the other concerns fall into their (much lower) place on the Things That Need My Immediate Attention Scale. Perhaps, as females, we can't stop thinking about the food (whether you are thinking about how much you want next or how much you shouldn't be having or how little you can get by on) because our spirit life is gnawing. Are we reaching for nachos to quiet the inner craving for communion with our Creator? Maybe we're exhibiting stringent control in our diets to avoid admitting that only God is sovereign and everything that happens (other than our chosen response) is out of our control. Could we be obsessing about our clothing to prevent anyone from knowing that we are spiritually naked under- neath it all? Questions like that make me want to grab a handful of Cheetos and run up the AmEx at Nordstrom.

Food is a wonderful thing. It nourishes us. It gives us fuel to do the things we need to do. It gives us an opportunity to sit down with people we love and discuss things that matter, and things that don't. It is one way we show our love and concern for people. As mothers we need to teach our daughters to respect and enjoy food. As daughters we need to receive food from our mothers knowing that it is given as a symbol of their love for us. You can diet on your own time. When you're with your mom, just eat. It will make you both feel better.

it came
from
hollywood

I didn't get to watch many Disney movies when I was a kid. It wasn't that my family was making a conscious effort to deprive me of my God-given-childhood-inalienable rights; it was simply a logistical issue. We grew up as Baptists and, back then, the way that you proved that you were tried-and-true-through-and-through-in-the-pew was to be present at your local neighborhood Baptist church every Sunday evening. This was, of course, a litmus test of your complete devotion to the Lord. If you were cutting church to watch *The Wonderful World of Disney* on a Sunday evening, you were suspect and placed on an unwritten list of People Who Need Watching. (There was another Super Litmus Test of the Saints: your attendance at the Wednesday night prayer service. If you were present and accounted for midweek then you were most assuredly saved. If you showed up for Monday night door-to-door witnessing you were doubtless Super Sanctified and were in a league all by yourself—sometimes literally.)

So, my childhood did not have a Disney theme. I did have

one Disney record of "Sleeping Beauty," which was almost as good as having seen it. I had a great imagination. So when my friends would discuss a Disney movie they had seen, I would normally catch enough of the plot to nod like I had seen it. And I could always count on a good Church of Christ girl to be fakin' along with me. They were the only kids who had more rules than the Baptists. Had technology experts invented TiVo thirty years earlier we would not have been forced to choose between communion and *The Wizard of Oz.*

My first entrée into the Disney entertainment machine came about when my kids were young and I was buying videos to amuse them while I was trying to get just about *anything* done. I was not the sort of mother who was above distraction. So I purchased all manner of Disney movies for my kids. After a while I started noticing a trend in the story lines: no mothers. Think about it. Most of the young girls in Disney films are motherless. Arielle (*The Little Mermaid*) — no mom. Belle (*Beauty and the Beast*) — no mom. *Cinderella* — she had a wicked stepmother, but no mom. Jasmine (*Aladdin*) — no mom. *Pocohantas* — no mom. Sure, Dumbo had a mom (he was separated from her), and Bambi had a mom (she got shot), but in general — not many moms living in Disneyland. It isn't until recently that there was a whole family represented in a Disney animation, and though they should have named them *The Exceptionals* they called them *The Incredibles.* In that movie the mom takes the term "stretch marks" to a whole 'notha level.

Things are not very realistic in TV Mom Land, either. In this magical place there are many different types of mothers on lots of shows, but in TV Mom Land the mothers never really lose it (with the exception of *Malcolm in the Middle's* mom — she loses it regularly). If there is a crisis it will always be resolved in exactly twenty-two minutes. Children are temporarily misbehaved but mostly charming. No one gets influenza bouts that require cleanup by a hazmat squad, has visible teenage acne, or gets held back a year in school. It's not real. But from the media moms who have become part of our collective social psyche, our culture has taken some of its cues and offered us a few bizarre lessons.

June Cleaver: Mother of Wally and the Beaver; wife of Ward.

Number of daughters — 0

June was the woman who made every REAL mom feel like a slouch. She found all things domestic to be utterly fascinating and always had a fresh-baked cookie awaiting her hungry schoolboys. She was perpetually freshly pressed and had at least one petticoat under her smart, trim skirt. Ever emotionally concerned, she made sure that husband Ward reconsidered his ways when he was "a little too hard on the Beaver" and was impervious to the relentless brownnosing of Eddie Haskell. She was Queen Bee of the Cleaver Clan and wielded her nifty fifties canister vacuum with a strand of pearls and an air of satisfaction.

> #1 Lesson of The June Cleaver School of Motherhood: Freshly baked cookies and well-vacuumed carpets make you dress better.

Shirley Partridge—Mom to all five of the little Partridges (no pear tree large enough, apparently, so they settled for a psychedelic bus): Keith, Danny, Laurie, Chris, and Tracy; widowed (it must have been either Danny's troublemaking or Keith's wardrobe budget that killed the dad).

Number of daughters—2

Shirley Partridge had to be one of the coolest moms in TV Land. She not only supported her children's dreams of forming a band, she actually believed that they could subsist on band gig pay. They were doing well enough to pay a manager, so we know this must be a Hollywood concocted fantasy. Shirley found that she could stand back and keyboard sync (smiling all the while!) as Keith always took the spotlight and Laurie played really bad tambourine. This is a mom who might have been slightly overinvolved in her children's lives. I mean, what teenager *wouldn't* want their mom in their band? C'mon!

> #1 Lesson in the Shirley Partridge School of Motherhood: Encourage your children to follow their dreams and, for Pete's sake, get off the stage.

Carol Brady—Mom to three very lovely girls, stepmom to three boys; wife of Mike.

I ask you, how hard could it be to be an attentive mom if you had Alice doing all of the cooking and cleaning and flirting with the butcher *for* you? What exactly *did* Carol Brady do with her days? I don't think I ever recall seeing her do anything of value.

Normally you see her sitting at a table or desk flipping through a magazine or cutting something out. What was she doing? Was she a compulsive coupon clipper? Was she the original Creative Memories Chick and we just weren't aware? I don't think we will ever know what she was doing, but we know that she had to spend much of her free time tending her ever-changing shag haircut. It must have been exhausting to keep just the right amount of flip from day to day.

> #1 Lesson from the Carol Brady School of Motherhood: Adore Husband #2, only stepparent boys, and hire loyal, snappy, less attractive help.

Maureen Robinson — Mother of Penny, Judy, and Will

If ever there was a television show devoted to the mother who has to make the best of a situation, which includes a dad with no GPS, the series *Lost in Space* qualifies as a guidebook for the long-suffering mom. She was trained as a biochemist and was to be the mom of the colony they were sent into weightlessness to populate. Through the nefarious doings of Dr. Zachary Smith they were blasted off course and forced to spend their days trying to figure out how to get home. Through all of this, TV mom Maureen kept a biochemically clean Jupiter II spaceship (she learned this on a prior TV show — she was little Timmy's mom in *Lassie*, after all). She spends a great deal of her free time looking for her kids (hence, the title "LOST in Space"). Of course having Robot to chant "Danger Will Robinson, Danger!" is the dream of every mom with a ten-year-old boy.

> #1 Lesson from the Maureen Robinson school of
> motherhood: If your man ever gets the family really,
> r-e-a-l-l-y lost you will be glad if you packed a lot of
> snacks and some kickin' technology (i.e., Robot) to
> keep the kiddos occupied.

Morticia Addams and Lily Munster—Somewhat interchangeable as they were both monster moms. Had husbands, had one of each kid, had various weird relatives living with them.

This is one of those Hollywood redundancy issues that make you wonder how audiences were expected to tell the shows apart. I certainly got them confused when I was growing up, but that's not saying much as I frequently confuse my own children.

Morticia and Lily were moms who saw their households as perfectly normal and worked hard to convince their children that all the *other* children's families were the strange ones. These moms put up with all manner of bizarre goings on inside the household and still aspired to community activism in spite of the fact that they were often maligned and misunderstood. They loved their men and cared for their offspring in their own weird Goth ways.

> #1 Lesson from The Monster Mom School of Motherhood: We're the only normal ones, honey.

Lucy Ricardo — Mom to Little Ricky; wife of Big Ricky.

Number of daughters — 0

Lucy was the stah, dahling — no room for a younger female. I heard that Vivian Vance was contractually required to stay plump in order to make Lucy look more glamorous. (I am going to tell everyone that I am contractually required to stay plump, too, in order to make my friends appear more glamorous. I'm just that kind of self-sacrificing friend.) We're not really sure if Little Ricky actually lived with Lucy or not. He was almost like a prop that they would drag out occasionally and then you wouldn't see him for a few weeks. My personal feeling is that Little Ricky had a secret stairway down to Fred and Ethel's place where he would camp out for weeks at a time, and Lucy was so consumed with launching her career that she never noticed. Little Ricky's main purpose for Lucy was to come out every now and again and bang on the drums for company, then off to bed (down the secret stairway to Fred and Ethel's, where Ethel would fuss over him and make him a peanut butter and jelly sandwich and he would smoke stogies with Fred). All well and good, unless Child Protective Services found out that he was living downstairs and then it would be, "Lucy, you got some 'splainin' to do."

> #1 Lesson of the Lucy Ricardo School of Motherhood: Talented children will find their own way in spite of having a dingbat for a mom.

Caroline Ingalls—Mother of three girls and one boy; wife of Charles.

This is a woman we could admire more if she weren't so perpetually okay about leaving behind her life Back East and braving the forces of nature as a homesteader. We occasionally see the danger and sacrifices that might mirror history, but she's mostly shown stirring pots on the stove, sewing by the lamp in her rocker (which Charles built for her by hand), and tucking in the children. We do not get to see her taking a morning trek to the freezing outhouse or gutting the possums that Charles killed for supper. The Little House women made do with what they had and tried to keep their feminine wits about them. It must have been hard to keep your corset cinched tightly and swing an ax. I once saw an Oprah show where she was living in a colonial life immersion experience for a week. She was not too excited when she found out that colonial era women did not wear bras or panties—but they did wear a corset. Hmmm . . . unsupported, breezy, *and* wasp-waisted. And we think the women of *our era* are overly vain? I think more women might have left the prairie if they didn't think they would be killed on the way back to civilization. But Caroline was a determined mother, determined to make sure her children were safe and educated and moral. On the prairie.

> #1 Lesson from the Caroline Ingalls School of Mother-hood: Should your family be moved to a new neighbor-hood with difficult conditions and hostile natives, you can still raise your children to be God fearin', literate

citizens. Besides, if your children see you successfully fighting off Indians they will be less likely to sass you.

Marion Cunningham—Mother to Richie and Joanie, honorary mother to The Fonz, Ralph Malph, and Potsie.

Happy Days mom "Mrs. C" was no fool. Though she spent a good deal of her time in the kitchen, it was primarily so she could hear what was going on in the living room with her kids and their friends. She was not afraid to stand in the gap and mother any creature that found its way under her roof. She had definite opinions about everyone's life and was not afraid to speak her piece. Mrs. Cunningham was a constant presence (much to her only daughter's chagrin) but made sure that everyone stayed connected and on the right track. She saw through Fonzie's tough-guy exterior and was the only one who got away with calling him "Arthur." She wasn't even too far gone to occasionally "get frisky" with Mr. C. What a gal.

> #1 Lesson from the Marion Cunningham School of Motherhood: It's not eavesdropping, it's "attentive listening."

Olivia Walton—Mother to a really big brood; wife of John.

Because I was an only child I recall thinking of Olivia Walton as a hero whenever I was enamored with all things Large Family. I envisioned myself as future Super Mom to my own brood of upstart writers, musicians, and scholars. The part I didn't envision was the unending state of pregnancy it takes to have a brood that large or the necessary accompanying poverty. Reality, indeed, bites. But when I was watching *The Waltons* on Thursday evenings it seemed like it was a simpler, better time. No matter that they were as poor as dirt and barely scraping by, they were a proud and close-knit clan that cared for one another and sacrificed to help each other. Olivia was a hard worker who was the emotional steadying force as her children navigated a wide range of issues due to the fact that they were spread out over twenty years. On any given day she could be encouraging John Boy to follow his dreams of becoming a writer and helping Elizabeth grieve over her deceased tadpole, both of seemingly equal in importance in Olivia's world. My personal favorite episode involved her going on strike when she felt that the rest of the family wasn't pulling their weight around the house. Way to go, girl! But I always felt a little sorry for her that she never worked up the courage to really tell Grandma off. You could cut the tension with a knife when those two were in the kitchen. It was always a race to see if the beans were going to get snapped before some*body* snapped. Didn't Grandma fall down a set of stairs in one of the episodes? Very suspicious if you ask me.

> #1 Lesson from the Olivia Walton School of Motherhood: Liquid assets could never compete with love assets.

Claire Huxtable—Mother of five (Sondra, Denise, Theo, Vanessa, Rudy); wife to Cliff.

On *The Cosby Show* Claire was The Mom Who Had it All: a loving, intelligent, available husband with a high-paying job; respectful kids; a great career as a lawyer; hip brownstone in the city; and apparently a law practice that demanded little of her after-hours hours. She was loving and tough with her kids and always willing to sit down and have a talk. If I were her kid I would have run far, far away when it was talking time. Hey—she's a lawyer. You know she's gonna lead you down a line of questioning designed to entrap you. Then she'll get you to admit to the crime you're accused of and— *bam!*—you're grounded. Case closed. But one of the things I most admired about her character was how she and Cliff always came up with creative discipline for their children. When Vanessa gets caught sneaking an alcoholic drink at a friend's house, they sit her down in their living room and ask her to play a drinking game with her little sister. Vanessa is horrified as it's Rudy's turn first—but then finds out that they are drinking tea instead of alcohol. Point made.

> #1 Lesson from the Claire Huxtable School of Motherhood: Law degrees help you win arguments, but creative love conquers all.

These fictional women sometimes set the bar too high. I mean, who could live up? They had writers—how many of us couldn't benefit from someone creating snappy comebacks and heartfelt emotional speeches for us to use with our kids? They had scripted husbands and scripted children. They had the benefit of "edit." Did a scene go badly? Edit. Miss a cue? Edit. Flub a line? Edit. Unfortunately we can't hit the "edit" button in our kids' minds. No, our children enshrine these moments and store them as monuments to our mothering inferiority. TV moms had musical soundtracks underscoring the highs and lows of their days. We have the music of the dishwashing machine swooshing in the background.

But no matter how impossible it is for Real Life Moms to measure up to the Hollywood Myth, we get the *real love*. Not always in the ways we might fantasize about, but unscripted and unedited. I'll take that lovin' spoonful over a TV dinner any day of the week.

actual results may vary

When you are a new mom you are fiercely conflicted about your mothering skills. There is within you a desire to live up to this new responsibility the very best that you can. You feel that you have absolutely no idea what you are doing at the same time you feel that no one else could do it any better.

When I had my first baby I just knew that I was going to hold him wrong or let his head flop back or do something that would damage him forever. I was a bundle of nervous insecurities. That was, until my mother-in-law came into the hospital room. My mother-in-law is a fine woman with plenty of experience with babies. She didn't do anything *wrong* with my baby, she was just holding him. But I felt this overwhelming urge to rip him from her arms. It was completely groundless and bizarre, yet it felt so strong. I was experiencing the internal conflict I like to call Novice/Expert Motherhood Syndrome: the deep knowledge that you don't know what you're doing *better* than anyone else.

This is the exact feeling that drives us to read parenting

columnists, listen to parenting radio shows, buy books on parenting, ask everyone's advice on parenting, Google parenting websites, commit chapter and verse of Dr. Spock or Dr. Dobson to memory, and go to any and every parenting seminar. We somehow believe that knowledge is power, and to some extent we are right. Parenting experts can give us some general guidelines as to the behavior tendencies and developmental markers that pertain to children in certain age ranges. They can suggest skills we can use to handle certain conflicts and crises. They can tell us what certain physical symptoms may indicate. They can point us to other experts in more specialized areas. What they cannot do, however, is give us the two things we need more than knowledge when we're parenting: the ability to relax and enjoy our child and the confidence to trust our intuition and instincts.

All these books and magazines and radio programs and seminars should have that itty bitty fine print that comes on every diet pill ad: "Actual results may vary." This is because motherhood doesn't involve any sort of certification. It doesn't seem logical that you must be certified to drive a car, lifeguard, open a hot dog stand, administer CPR, or go fishing, but you're freely permitted to give birth and raise a child from scratch. No kind of license or training required. Apparently anyone with ovaries and a willing partner can have a child. Society just throws you in the deep end of the pool and smiles and waves, "You'll do fine!"

When we left the hospital with our firstborn, we were given a week's supply of diapers and formula and a nose syringe. That was it. Like the most important thing about motherhood has to do with plugging up the mouth hole, unplugging the nose hole, and keeping things clean and dry down south. I was hoping for some sort of manual for this little person, but the discharge papers only had instructions for me.

As we were driving away from the hospital I was overcome with sheer panic. A thousand what ifs raced through my hormonal brain, and I can't say that I came up with even one that I felt sure I could handle. The nurses told me how to care for the navel (lots of alcohol on it 'til the little stump falls off) but not how to tell if Calvin was really sick and needed a doctor's attention. I wished I had figured out a way to stay at the hospital a little longer and asked the important questions of qualified medical professionals. Alas, no. I was in the deep end and it was time to swim.

As a first-time mom, I felt that the more information I could get the better parent I would be. So I started reading everything I could get my hands on to make sure that I had all the bases covered. What I didn't know was that many of the "experts" disagreed with each other, and they all argued convincingly for their theories. Some said to hold your baby and comfort your baby as much as was physically possible. Others said that would be spoiling the baby and giving him or her too much power in the household. "Lay them down and let them cry it out and comfort themselves." I don't know how other moms did that, but I never could. What were they going to use to comfort themselves? Recent pleasant in utero memories?

John and I looked to various experts on colic treatment (wind up swings vs warm baths?), the best diaper regimen (powder vs ointment? Aloe wipes vs alcohol? Cloth vs disposable?), appropriate soothers (pacifiers vs thumbs?). It didn't take us long to amass quite a collection of pacifiers. We had them in every room of our house, in the diaper bag, in the car, in the fridge, in drawers, on windowsills, in between the couch cushions — I mean *everywhere.* Yet, amazingly, we could rarely find one when we desperately needed it. It would become like our own little indoor Easter Egg Hunt at 3 a.m. (I have a theory about this: I suspect that all the lost pacifiers are hanging out on some beach with all the single socks that got lost in the dryer.)

There was also the diaper deal. Because we were trying to do everything the best way we could we started out using cloth diapers. I had this idealized fantasy that I would be outside hanging all these sparkling white rectangles on a clothesline where they would wave in the breeze like banners as a testament to my motherhood superiority. I, unlike The Lesser Mothers, was devoted to purity and wholesomeness on my baby's bottom. I, unlike The Lesser Mothers, was willing to sacrifice for the health of my child and the good of our environment.

I, unlike The Lesser Mothers, was tragically uninformed. It took only one (stinkin') week of superiority and rinsing those things out in the toilet (eeeeewwwww) for me to realize that disposable diapers were God's gift to modern mothers. I have to give props to the women who came before us who did the diaper washing routine for years. This could have been why people used to be so adamant about early potty training.

I decorated the nursery. I have no idea why, other than I saw people on TV doing it. This was a total waste of time since none of my children ever slept or played in their nurseries. They were attached to *me* the whole time. (Obviously you have to hire a "nurse" to make that whole nursery thing work.) I also bought the whole line of reasoning that the more baby stuff you had the better mom you were. So we had it all—crib, bassinet, layette, stroller, car seat, Pack-n-Play portable baby bed—you name it, we had it. What we soon came to realize is that, when it was time to go somewhere, we had to be strapped to the top of the car since, after packing in all that necessary stuff, there was no room for us.

I now know the truth: that little babies can sleep almost anywhere with a couple of pillows propped on either side of them so they won't roll off. (Mother's Little Secret #101: Most children will roll off something before they are five years old. They live.) All the great pains we took to "childproof" the house were before we realized that children do not understand this concept and appreciate a good challenge while trying to fall down stairs/open dangerous cabinets/get electrocuted.

I remember the time we had to take our firstborn to get his first round of immunizations. I felt like a crumb because I was holding my precious little innocent baby while some nurse who looked like she just left the World Wrestling Federation's training program stuck him with a needle. As an "educated" parent I knew it was necessary and would ultimately protect him from childhood diseases, but when you are holding your child while he is getting stuck it feels like you are going against the Motherhood Geneva Conventions.

And nothing is worse for a mom than to see her child suffer. We just don't deal well. It goes against our Mother Bear nature. Besides the routine immunization appointments, I remember the time my first child had croup. (For the uninitiated croup is a condition that involves the inflammation of the upper airway that leads to a cough that sounds like a bark, sort of like a seal.) Being a novice mom I reasoned that putting my baby in a steamy bathroom would help him breathe. Duh. The heat made the inflammation worse and his breathing almost impossible. As my husband was out of town I called a neighbor to take us to the hospital in the middle of the night. I was frantic. It was in January and I bundled us up and loaded us in our (sweet) neighbor's car. Much to my surprise within about three minutes Calvin was breathing much better. (This also supports my theory that the moment you decide that things are serious enough to warrant a trip to the doctor, the germs know that you mean business and back off. This is why your child appears symptom-free by the time you reach the doctor's office.) Little did I know that cold air is what causes the breathing passages to return to normal.

Experience: that thing you get just after the moment you needed it.

Recently I picked up a copy of Malcolm Gladwell's book *Blink* and, after reading it, wished that it had been around when my children were little. Gladwell contends that we are able to "thin slice" information and that our gut is quite reliable when it comes to making important decisions. He says that we don't need more information, we just need to think intuitively about the information we already possess. I have heard many anecdotal instances of mothers bringing their children to the doctor based on a feeling that "something just wasn't right" — only to be told by the doctor that they were wise to do so as the child was on the verge of something very serious and got there "just in time." So whaddya know: It's just like Dr. Spock wrote in *Baby and Child Care* back in 1945: "Trust yourself. You know more than you think you do."

We can read every parenting advice book, attend seminars, collect folders full of information, and ask our friends for the benefit of their experience, but eventually we find out that our kids are not "projects" to be fixed and improved and renovated and built for the display of our superior parenting skills. Rather, they are entrusted treasures (okay — so they don't come fully loaded with good manners and life skills, but they're treasures nonetheless.). We are responsible for doing the best we can, loving them the most we can, investing in them in every way we can, but the actual results are not ours to determine. Those are in God's hands.

I did eventually figure out a few things on my own. One was that almost all packaging is more interesting than the toy it holds. I have no idea why this piece of information is absent from the child-rearing books, but all young mothers should know this. I also found out that kids can figure out how to get along as soon as a mom makes the ground rule that, unless someone is bleeding or something is on fire, absolutely no tattling. I also learned to never, *ever* let my kids play with Scotch Tape. That is, unless I had an important phone call. If I needed to keep my kids quiet for a good long time I could count on a roll of sticky tape in my hour of need. I found it to be a wonderful secret weapon. But like all great weapons it should be used only as absolutely necessary and when a mom is ready to deal with the fallout afterward. Scotch Tape, after all, sticks to stuff. And if you leave a child alone with it for very long, lots of it will be stuck to lots of stuff—which may be why this particular piece of advice does not appear in any childr-earing books.

I'm not sure what the qualifications for "expert" are in the area of child-rearing, but if you happen to see a woman who has more than a couple of kids and the kids seem well-mannered, kind, and happy, and if the woman has on clothes that match and has styled her own hair in the front *and* the back, and she isn't yelling at anyone, she just might be an expert. And you can ask her how she's doing it. But remember—actual results may vary.

all i * really want

Another theory (I have a lot of them): I think adolescent girls are maturing physically faster than they ever have. My hypothesis is that this is due, in part, to the bovine growth hormone that ranchers give to cows to make them make more milk and the hormones they give chickens to make them have unnaturally large breasts. If you think about the amount of milk or chicken nuggets your daughter eats it might explain why you are shopping for a larger bra size than you purchased at the same age. Life seems like it happens faster these days and kids get to do everything younger than we did when we were growing up. I didn't get a cell phone until I was in my late twenties; Elyse got one for her thirteenth birthday. I didn't have a passport until I was thirty; Elyse got one when she was nine. I hope this doesn't mean that she'll hit menopause when she's twenty-five.

My daughter and I went to see the Disney movie *Freaky Friday* a few years ago. Lindsay Lohan's character repeats to her mother over and over, "I hate you! You are ruining my life!" Of course, neither was true, but it feels true when you are that age. And it is every mother's secret fear—that she actually *is* ruining her daughter's life, but that the damage won't show up for years and then it will be too late. This fear sometimes leads us to project strength and perfection onto our daughters—and that wall only separates us more.

A sore subject during my adolescent years was The Rules of Dating. Every family has them. They vary from family to family and some are stricter than others. Being an only child was probably a disadvantage in this regard; I was not allowed to single date until I was a *senior* in high school! Of course this seemed like The Most Unfair Rule of all, since all my friends could date at sixteen. My dad used to joke that he would send me to a Baptist convent if only they existed. I did not find this funny. I was allowed to go on church-group outings or on chaperoned dates with my parents (no, thank you), so The Rule was very effective. I did not single date until I was eighteen.

I used to listen to my parents explain The Rule to me over and over, but no matter how they couched it, it still sounded like their chief purpose was to ruin my life. When I was in the middle of a heated discussion with my mom, I can remember looking at her and thinking, "What do you want from me?! I'm already voted 'Most Likely to Pray at Baccalaureate.' If you are trying to make me the Last Living Non-Dater on earth, you are succeeding!"

But now, as a mother of my own girl who is sticking one toe into adulthood, I know that the better question would have been, "What do you want *for* me?" Not that I would have been able to imagine an answer to that question *then*, but *now* I can see how my mom just wanted me to be old enough to handle the pressure that the whole dating thing brings with it. She wanted me to continue to focus on my own maturity rather than being distracted by thoughts of who-liked-me-how-much-and why-not. She wanted me to be healthy and happy. That's what all mothers want.

Even in the Bible we are witness to moms who want things for their kids—the women who brought their children to Jesus to be healed or blessed, the mother of James and John who didn't want much (just that her sons would have starring-role seats on the right and the left side of Jesus when he came into His kingdom). Moms really can't help this desire to have the very best for their widdle dumplings. We may sometimes be misdirected but we are usually well-intentioned.

There is so much I want for my daughter—things I desperately want her to experience and experiences I desperately want her to avoid. I want her life to be rich and full, yet I know that richness is meaningless without blinding moments of pain that give way to wisdom and clarity. So here is my list of things I want for her. (I have considered doing a video of me reciting this list so that, in the middle of our next moment of "intense fellowship" I can hit the Play button to remind her of my noble intentions.)

ALL I REALLY WANT FOR YOU IS:

   . . . an unshakable sense that you are unique, valuable, kissed by God.

   . . . that you know you are loved by us no matter what.

   . . . to know that you always have other options.

. . . the certainty that your dad and I could not be prouder to be your parents.

. . . for you to look in the mirror and like what you see.

. . . that you can lay your head down every night with a clear conscience.

. . . for you to know that your worth is never dependent on a man.

. . . that you can accomplish anything God puts in your heart to do.

. . . friends who will reflect your strengths and gently reveal areas of weakness.

. . . friends who make you laugh and will let you have a good cry.

. . . a strong sense of a calling that goes beyond a paycheck.

. . . the ability to spot posers and predators a mile away (because you don't need to be any closer to them than that).

. . . a good idea of when something is over and the ability to close the door and move on when it's time.

. . . a healthy respect for money coupled with the knowledge that stuff does not contain happiness molecules.

. . . a closet that has minimal purchase mistakes so that every item is worthy of the inch allotted to it.

. . . a memory brimming with experiences that keep widening your world.

. . . enough challenge in your life to keep you flexible.

. . . for you to have the good sense to ask "what?" instead of "why?"

. . . that you will always pay attention to how you feel and what you are feeling because emotions are a gift—feel them, but don't make important decisions based solely on them.

. . . a love of a good meal and great conversation.

. . . the ability to celebrate everything.

. . . the confidence to speak up when you need to and to leave things unsaid that won't change anything.

. . . deep contentment no matter what the checkbook balance says.

. . . to know how much time it takes to get things done and the discipline to do it.

. . . time for poor people, old people, and children.

. . . the ability to calm your own self down.

. . . a childlike wonder that remains with you until you're 100 years young.

. . . the hope and encouragement that comes from knowing that tomorrow brings a brand new bucket of fresh mercy (see Lamentations 3:22-23).

And really, though my "want for" list looks long, is it so much for a mother to ask?

playing favorites

I've heard it before.

"Wow. It must've been difficult being an only child."

"Do you ever regret not having brothers or sisters?"

"Weren't you lonely being an only child?"

I rarely even try to explain, but being an only child does have its advantages. I mean, I never had to worry about who would get the most Christmas presents (me!), who would have the most privileges (me, again!), or who was Mom's favorite (always me!). My aunts and uncles wondered if I was ever going to be able to get along with others if I never had to share a bedroom or bathroom or parent. They were just jealous.

Of my mom's sisters and brothers, I was the only one among my cousins who was an Only, so I had a front row seat to All Things Sibling through my cousins' families. I saw how they loved and despised each other, stood up for and picked on each other, formed alliances and excluded each other, and how they compared everything the other got. I had enough cousins to stand in as substitute brothers and sisters until we moved away from my hometown when I was twelve.

If any woman ever prayed, "Dear God, I just want to be the center of someone's universe," this prayer takes on whole new meanings when you have more than one child. You are not only the center of more than one person's universe, but now you are also placed under a microscope where your every move and motive is scrutinized and analyzed to determine if the love quotient is equal for all. I have a theory that several of the founding fathers of our country must have been middle children as much as they were champions of absolute equality.

Whenever there was something to be split up among our kids, my husband and I adopted the "one divide, one choose" rule. Under this construct, whatever was to be divvied up was put out and one of the kids got to split it, but the measurer had to let the non-measurers be the first to choose. You can imagine that it was divided with an eye to mere *millimeters* when it was done with that rule in mind!

As much as that procedure helped out with things like chocolate cake and the last chicken strip, it set a dangerous precedent for other areas like Christmas presents. You can try as hard as you want to spend the exact same amount on each child (some moms even get down to the penny, purchasing an extra piece of bubble gum so that everything will be "fair"), but the problem is that *kids don't read the receipts* and they will still perceive that someone else in the family is more delighted than they are with their gift. I've tried to instill in my kids that we are shooting for equal gifting over a lifetime, not with every birthday or holiday. Sometimes it's just your year—everything you had on your Christmas wish list was on sale! Sometimes the price tag for your new set of car tires means you get tube socks and Fruit Roll-Ups. Of course this is antithetical to the spirit of the "splitter doesn't get to be first chooser" rule, but consistency in parenting is overrated.

Unfortunately in human relationships it's not really possible to get totally precise in how the affection and attention is distributed among your babies. No matter how careful you try to be, someone is going to perceive that they are on the short end of the Parental Love Stick.

It would be great if there was a time for each child when they would get to be the Only for a little while. When any of our kids got to be the only kid at home for a while they turned into different people than when they were thrown into the normal mix. It was interesting to observe how they relaxed about things when their Perceived Injustice Microscope was unplugged for a week or so. Unfortunately it never lasted, since their siblings came back from wherever they had been and the hunt for evidence of favoritism resumed.

If there's more than one child, it seems that the more melancholic-tempered one will always be on the lookout for verification that they are not the favorite. On the hit sitcom *Everybody Loves Raymond*, Brad Garrett's character, policeman Robert (Ray's younger, TALLER brother) spent nine seasons spouting evidence that Ray was the most favored child of the family. One classic: "Everybody loves Raymond. When I go to work, people shoot at me. When Ray goes to work, people do the wave."

On any given day you could ask any of your children to come up with a list of things that prove they are the favorite, and they might be able to come up with two or three entries if they sat and thought about it for hours. Ask them to come up with a list of things that proves any *other* child in the family is the favorite and they could fill two legal pads, single spaced, multiple columns in about ten minutes.

What's a mom to do? Of course you love all your children — but equally? Is that even possible? Come on, you love them all, but you love them *differently*— uniquely. Psychologists differ on why we find it easier to express love or get along with certain children and not others. Do we get along better with the ones we identify with (personality-wise) because we understand them better? Or do they get under our skin more easily because we see ourselves in them and we don't like what we see? If we take some time to examine each of our children and the way we feel about them deep down (not in the sanitized, politically correct, "I-love-them-all-the-same" mode), we might be able to deal honestly with why our kids might feel that someone in the family is Favorite and how we may be engendering that perception by our actions.

As a daughter you can't really have a favorite mom. You only get the one you get. That doesn't mean that you don't spend time fantasizing that all your friends must have better moms than you have. You are just absolutely convinced that every mom has to be cooler, looser, hipper, more normal than yours. This is the familiarity/contempt problem that gets solved rather quickly with a weekend sleepover at another mother's house. It seems that, from afar, every mom looks slightly superior to the one you have. Once you spend more than twenty-four hours in your friend's household, however, you discover that every mom knows those same, worn phrases that your mom uses on you, and the other mother has hormones, too.

Dr. Gary Chapman has several books out dealing with the issue of "love languages." He contends that we all have a way that we like to receive love and that is our "love language." For some it's words, for others it's gifts, for some it's affection, for others it's quality time or acts of service. The problem that arises from this is that we usually prefer to *give* love in the language in which we like to *receive* it. If all of your children had the same love language as you do, all would be bliss and everyone would feel equally loved. But if your child has a love language that differs from yours you may be shouting, "I love you" in your language and your child may not be able to translate at all. This kind of disconnect can be discouraging at best and long-term scarring if allowed to continue.

Elyse and I have one love language in common—we both like presents. I like surprises. She doesn't. I think it is a wonderful serendipity to be given something that you weren't expecting. She wants to be able to choose it. (I raised her to be particular . . . now I'm reaping.) When I bring her something I picked out for her it doesn't make her feel valued and loved, it makes her feel that I am imposing my taste upon her. So I am learning to watch when I am with her for things that make her heart sing so that I will *know* which thing she wants instead of supposing that I know her taste and preference.

Unfortunately, this is not her primary love language. I say "unfortunately" because it would be tricky (but still do-able) to provide a pretty steady stream of happy little delights for her. That would just take money. But my daughter's primary love language is in the area of time and attention. She longs to have me park myself on the couch with her and talk about anything and nothing and everything for a while. This does not take money—it takes time. I deeply value the fact that Elyse wants to talk to me (some mothers would give anything if their daughter wanted to talk to them) but, as I am a do-er, it's hard for me to plop myself down and stay there for very long. We do make it happen every now and again, but most of the time she comes up to my bathroom while I'm soaking in the tub or crawls up in my bed and we talk. I am praying for her future husband. I will know him when I see him—he will be the one with big ear canals.

When the writer of Proverbs instructs us to "train up a child in the way he should go" there is the implication that we study our children, understand their particular uniqueness, and discern how they receive love best. Then it is our privilege to show love to each child in such a way that they can hear it loud and clear. And what a tragedy to have a child in your home for the formative years of their life and not to be interested enough in their heart to find the key.

This is emotional laziness at its worst, and it happens between mothers and daughters more than anyone would care to admit. We dig our heels in on either side and say, "Well, I am who I am and I can't give her any more than that." Partly true, partly hogwash. The true part is that we are who we are. We all come hardwired

with traits and bents and personality quirks. This makes us bless-
edly unique. But the hogwash part is when we act as though that
gives us the right to deny affection (because it is hard to learn a
new love language) or run roughshod over each other (because
we presume that the love and grace will always be available in
unlimited supply). We create an emotional climate that ultimately
dishonors one another under the guise of "authenticity."

Wouldn't it be wonderful if every daughter felt that she held
her own place of "favoritism" in her mother's heart? If you are a
mother I ask you to consider what you could say to your daughter
to help her feel that. And what if every mother felt as though she
were the only mother her daughter ever wanted? If you are a daughter I ask you to consider expressing your love for her in a way that
would honor her. By embracing each other's uniqueness and learning to give love in a way that the other can receive it we can begin
to change the way we receive it. It's never too late to start.

moms
of the
bible

If you have spent your adult life trying to live up to the mothering standard set in the thirty-first chapter of Proverbs (and I know some women do), you might as well just go ahead and take up permanent residence in the I-Can't-Quite-Measure-Up Lane. I have a sneaking suspicion that that woman was either a composite sketch of several stellar women, a wishful hope, or a case of one woman mistakenly believing her own press kit.

The intro to that chapter of Proverbs states that these are "the sayings of King Lemuel—an oracle that his mother taught him." Webster defines this sort of oracle as "a person giving wise or authoritative decisions or opinions." I would amend that to say that this was likely a mother hoping none of the girls her son was currently dating would ever measure up to her "oracle." Regardless, we are left with the impression that this sort of mother is the Approved Standard Version—family centered, good business woman, great cook, generous, prepared, discreet, praiseworthy, wise, and beautiful. If she was indeed a real woman—all things to all people and extraordinarily perfect—then I'm just glad we didn't have a chance to meet. She could never have considered me as part of her Potential Friend Pool.

This is precisely why I am so glad that the Bible gives us pictures of other kinds of mothers—the ones who cause us to nod our head to affirm the phrase, "If you can't be a good example then you'll just have to be a horrible warning." I have come up with examples of a few of both types in the following list. There are many other moms in God's Word, but these are a sampling of the good, the bad, and the downright bizarre.

EVE: The Original Mother—more specifically, of Cain, Abel, and Seth (and several unnamed others).

I guess if we are to commence in chronological order we would have to begin with Eve, the mother of us all. And she was the woman who made THE monumental, mind-blowing, affects-everybody-forever mistake. So she probably deserves the bad rap she gets. But it wasn't like there were any other women around to make it instead of her, right? Maybe she was the first to partake of the fruit just because she was the only one who could remember where it was in the garden (women just know where stuff is). You have to feel a little bit of sympathy for the girl who didn't have a mother to ask about how things were for her back in the day. When the kids had a temperature or were teething she just had to figure it out on her own, but, then again, nobody could look at her and tell her that she was doing it all wrong. And sure, she got us into epidurals, but she had the mother of all heartache, too. Her sons were involved in the first homicide (without Nintendo and violence on TV to blame it on). She was the first mom to have to bury her child.

SARAH: Mother of Isaac.

This is the mom who gives hope to everyone who waited a little late to get started on the Mommy Track. Not that she didn't try; her womb was just on a different biological clock. God made a promise to Abraham that he would be the father of many nations. This led Sarah to the logical conclusion that she would be the mother of many nations. When that wasn't happening in a timely manner, Sarah decided to do her own thang, so to speak. She gave her hand maiden Hagar as her maternal stunt double. This resulted in *a* child but not *the* child. When the messenger of the Lord told Abraham that it really would be Sarah that was going to deliver the promised baby, Sarah overheard, laughed, and promptly got in trouble for it. But if you were her age you would laugh, too, just thinking about how the breast-feeding would be easy now that she could just lay Isaac on her lap to do it. Sarah is a sister who could laugh at her late start with motherhood knowing that good things come to those who wait.

REBEKAH: Mother of Jacob and Esau.

For every mom who has ever had the temptation to play favorites with her children, pay attention to Rebekah. She didn't just play favorites, she schemed and connived and was an accessory to one of the biggest Daddy Dupes in all of history. It says it plain in Scripture that Isaac loved Esau because he was an outdoorsman but Rebekah loved Jacob. This kind of favoritism does not bode well for a family. When the lines are drawn and it is obvious who is thick with whom, life can get very messy. Rebekah was in collusion with Jacob (even his name meant "trickster") to take the birthright from his older brother. I'm sure she rationalized that it wasn't such a bad thing since the twin boys were only separated by moments, but her hand in helping Jacob trick his father was her way of thumbing her nose at the order of things and a diss to her dying husband. Turns out that this family rift lasted for a long time. Rebekah reminds us that it is a dangerous thing to use maternal power for manipulation.

BATHSHEBA: Mother of Solomon.

Bathsheba was well-named as it was her "bath-ing" that attracted the attention of King David. Their illicit affair resulted in the birth of a son. David tried for some damage control by sending her husband out to war, back to the house hoping for a copulating cover-up, and then out to the frontlines to get killed. (And we think we have seriously evil plots in *our* current movies.) David got his wish — Bathsheba's husband was killed in battle, and David thought he had gotten away with it. Nathan confronted him and David repented bitterly. But we never really hear how it all affected Bathsheba. Their sin is well documented and the effects to David's household long-lasting. However, a son was born from their union and Solomon turned out to be a peaceable ruler whose wisdom was legendary. Bathsheba's motherhood gives women hope that, regardless of the circumstances surrounding your pregnancy and the birth of your child, God can redeem any situation. You never know, you might just have the wisest person ever on the planet staring back at you from that high chair.

JOCHEBED: Mother of Aaron, Moses, and Miriam.

If there was ever a mom whose life would have made a great screenplay for a Lifetime for Women movie it would be Jochebed. You just have to give it up for her and the midwives who, in their act of civil disobedience, allowed Moses to be born. Those midwives, when asked by the pharaoh why they were not killing the boy babies as commanded, replied that the Hebrew women were "too vigorous" and popped those babies out before they could get there! Thus baby Moses was born but had to be sent down the river (literally) with his sister serving as lookout, only to be pulled out of the water by the pharaoh's daughter, who secured the services of Moses' biological mom to nanny him. Talk about movie script material! Oh wait. They've already done that. Anyway, Moses' mom shows us that the determination and ingenuity of a desperate mother can result in surprising circumstances. Oh, the places you'll go!

MARY: Mother of Jesus.

Talk about your Personal EPT . . . I mean Mary's was early, EARLY! And accurate, too. Angelic visitation definitely qualifies as a sure thing. But the favored girl had to have some concerns because unwed pregnancy was a little different back then. You could get stoned for it. I'm sure she was very relieved to find out that the angel had given her beau, Joseph, the same message. And yes, she was going to give birth to the divine Gift of heaven, but, as any mother knows, all gifts come with some work attached. She still had to change the Baby Jesus' diapers, soothe him as he teethed, teach him to walk, and clean up his skinned knees. She had to cook the meals and wash his clothes and do all the things that moms do for their children. It's interesting the places we see Mary pop up in the gospels—for example, at the temple sending out an APB for her boy. (I believe I might have grounded Jesus if he told me that he was just doing his father's business, but no such reaction from Mary is recorded.) Another of my favorite mother moments of Mary's was when she was at the wedding feast apparently exasperated with her thirty-year-old son for not doing that "thing" he could do with the water. When Jesus seems to refuse to come through the way she knows he can, she goes around him and tells the servants to get ready to do something for him. And Jesus does the miracle. I would have loved to have been there to see the looks pass between mother and son that night. And then we see Mary at the crucifixion. Disciples may scatter, followers may be in hiding, but a mother stays when the rest of the world walks away. In fact, Mary is a rich tapestry of real motherhood: a lot of excitement followed by years of work and moments of intense pain. But through it all, mothers are there.

These moms in the Bible reveal to us that mother-love is fierce and stubborn to a fault—even wrong-headed sometimes. We do right things for wrong reasons and wrong things because we think everyone needs our help. When you look at the moms in the Bible say a silent prayer of thanks that these women are included alongside the Oracle of Lemuel in Proverbs 31 to bring snapshots of reality and spiritual caution cones to our journey.

other
mothers

I remember when Hillary Clinton's book *It Takes a Village* came out several years back, the accompanying uproar from conservatives was deafening. Many people saw it as a communal manifesto for socialism—where society takes over raising our children and we give up our parental power. I have to confess that I've never read her book. I might have been too busy raising my kids to read about all the people it takes to raise kids. But regardless of what you think of Hillary, her book, or her politics, the girl was sorta right in this one regard: If you are born female it certainly does take a lot of mothers in your life to be fully mothered and well-mothered.

As a mother it is hard for me to admit that there might be something my daughter needs in her life that my limited experience or expertise can not provide for her, but I truly believe that no one should have to mother alone. I am one (primary and important) mothering voice in the ear of my daughter. My mother was a constant, formative voice in my life and remains so to this day. Do I believe that my mother had everything I needed for my total development as I came to adulthood? Or do I think I have the corner on all the female perspective that my daughter will need to get through her life? I do not. Because we are all in some way emotionally handicapped we cannot provide everything that our daughters will need. I know that my mother's guidance was important to me, but I also had the input of my mother *and* grandmothers and aunts and family friends and mentors.

I am old enough to recall when you could get in trouble everywhere in your town by any female adult who felt motherly toward you. If someone caught you doing anything immoral, illegal, disrespectful, or even *questionable,* they were not deterred by the fact that they did not share your particular strand of DNA. Wrong was wrong, and if you were wrong, they felt a social obligation to step in and mother you correctionally. This might have involved giving you a good talking to, possibly applying some immediate form of discipline and assuring you that, should you choose not to voluntarily confess to your own mother upon your arrival at the house, your mom *would be told.* And this was followed by a burning up of the party lines (for those of you under the age of forty, skip it—party lines are too hard to explain) faster than the speed of light so that, when you did arrive home, it was old news and your mom already had her speech ready and some form of discipline lined up. You could waste your breath explaining, but the shame of someone else catching you misbehaving was unbearable for her. It was now her job to make it equally unbearable for you. That was the downside of a community full of mothers.

The upside was that you could also have a cadre of women

who would love, support, and encourage you in areas where your own mother did not have a background for input. This is the aspect of having Other Mothers that allows young women to excel and spread their wings beyond their own heritage. Sometimes it's easy to discount the praise or encouragement of your own mother because you are suspect that it is so motivated by love that it isn't exactly objective. This is the fault of a mother gene that can see beauty and potential when neither may be obvious to others. But when women who are not bound to you by relational duty look into your life and tell you that you are gifted you tend to listen to and believe them primarily *because* they aren't your mom.

I believe it is a tragedy that we are losing our sense of this in our society. There used to be a time when you could be mothered not only by your own mom but also by a stepmom, your grandma, your auntie, your school teacher (or lunch lady or school nurse), your Sunday school teacher, your friend's mom, and even your mother-in-law. In some church cultures they appoint "church mothers," and these powerful, God-fearin' women are deputized to ask you embarrassing questions, rebuke you if they see that your life is on the wrong track, and basically get up in your business. *All* up in your business. It's their spiritual imperative.

My friend Skip is a spiritual mother. She is single and has no biological children, but she has many people who look to her for wisdom and guidance. One special relationship with someone who asked her to step in and help her to heal from the estrangement from her biological mother has been particularly rewarding. Skip's "daughter of choice" is a woman whose life looks very different from her own, but they have mutually chosen to enter into this relationship and have the freedom to be honest with each other at all times.

Skip was an adopted child and describes her own mother as godly, faith-filled, rock solid, gracious, and tied in to her community as she taught school for decades and kept up with her students through the years. Many of these same traits can be said of Skip, and her life purpose is to nurture believers into mature disciples. Her own mother's example coupled with Skip's vocational choices (she is a nurse, speaker, author, and life coach) point to her love for helping people. But when Skip was approached about being a spiritual mother to a younger friend her first reaction was reluctance. She couldn't really see how this would work over the long term. But as their bond grew deep, Skip realized that "spiritual mother/daughter relationship" more accurately defined what was happening than anything else. Skip explains the difference this way: "Mentoring is 'Here is the way, follow me.' Life coaching is 'Let me come alongside you and help you find the way.' Spiritual mothering is 'Come sit on my lap.' Total access."

Sometimes your Other Mother is there out of necessity. My mom's mom was my first Other Mother. Nana wasn't highly educated in book learnin' (I think she may have finished the eighth grade) but she had done her "post grad" in The School of Hard Times and had her honorary doctorate in How the World Works. The great thing about spending time with your grandmother is that, (1) She thinks you are The Cheese, and (2) She is the only one who knows all the dirt on your mom. As hard as it is for you to imagine the woman who gives you The Business getting into trouble herself, you are spending quality time with the woman who gave your mom The What For on a regular basis. This could explain the unspoken bond between grandmothers and grandchildren. Grandmothers are powerful. I am planning to use this power whenever I have grandchildren of my own. I have already ordered those T-shirts for kids that say, "What happens at Grandma's stays at Grandma's."

I was privileged to have two very different types of grandmothers in my developing years. I had my Nana in Texas, and when my mother remarried I got the bonus of another type of grandmother. Ludie Pulliam had definitely finished higher than eighth grade; in fact she was a chemist who was chosen to work on the development of the hydrogen bomb during World War II. Their family relocated to Los Alamos when my stepfather was young, and their life was quite different from Nana's. Ludie had a housekeeper and cook and worked her entire adult life as a scientist until she retired and moved back to Laurel, Mississippi, to be near her family. She was my grandmother who loved sports, card games, and frying shrimp. My Nana didn't know the first thing about sports, considered playing cards a sin, and never peeled a shrimp in her life. But my life is the richer for the diversity of my grandmothers. I am grateful that my daughter is experiencing the same thing with her grandmothers. My mom loves all things domestic and John's mom loves all things educational. Elyse has one of each: a cooking grandmother and a read-aloud grandmother. That doesn't mean that either could not do both, but why not just let everyone flow in their areas of giftedness?

Nana died when I was eighteen years old. As a mother of nine children, Nana's health started declining in her early fifties. All the women that she mothered (daughters, granddaughters, nieces, daughters-in-law, friends) grieved the passing of a woman who felt no higher calling than to serve and encourage others. My mom told me that she felt protective of her mother all of her life because my grandmother's health was already in decline by the time my mom was old enough to help around the house. So in her own way, my mother felt motherly toward her mother. But my mom does not recall ever having any feelings of angst or resentment toward her mother, mostly protective feelings toward Nana. This is the way it works with mothers and daughters. Complexity and tangled feelings can flip the script and keep things emotionally out of order. Regardless of the situation, the mother/daughter bonds are fierce and powerful and leave an enormous tear when one leaves this earth.

As my mom was only thirty-nine when her mother died she was left motherless as she was approaching middle age. It has been interesting to watch her choose her own Other Mothers. In the years since Nana's passing my mom has sought out and continued to stay in contact with various women who were friends of her mother and has allowed these women who knew her mother to mother her. It has been comforting to her to be in relationship with these women. But she did not wait for these Other Mothers to come into her life. She sought them out, made regular phone calls, kept up with their health care, sent cards, and stayed involved in their lives. Sometimes you have to go beyond your comfort level to get the comfort you need.

There is a special group of women who are thrust into Other Mother status because they remarry. These women are stepmoms. Of all the Other Mothers, this role requires the most patience, tenacity, and understanding. The children of the first marriage feel that the entrance of the stepmom signals the death of the first family, so they can't help but view her with distrust and suspicion. Stepmoms are often perceived as intruders, unwanted love-stealers interloping through a house of hurt, trying to build new relationships with children who don't even want her there, much less in their lives. I have seen some navigate with grace and others crack beneath the incredible strain of being rejected day after day. God bless the stepmothers of the world. Theirs is a difficult row to hoe.

Then there are the mothers-in-law, the women who raise the men we marry. To them we owe a debt of gratitude for raising a son who knew a good thing when he saw it! I know there are a million mother-in-law jokes, but there are also a million mothers-in-law who love and befriend their daughters-in-law. I am thankful for Vesta and her love for John. When she recounts stories of John's life pre-me, I feel that I am getting an important glimpse into the events that shaped him into the man I came to love. Of course your mother-in-law's ways are different from your household of origin and that's exactly what makes her a valuable Other Mother in your life. Without her perspective you may never fully understand what makes your man tick. Allow your mother-in-law her own special place among your Other Mothers and let her know that she is appreciated.

I recall some of my own Other Mothers. I had high school

teachers who went beyond their classroom duties to encourage me in the arts, and I have had women who have taken me under their wings to give me wisdom from their journey when it was of no apparent benefit to them, but just because they wanted to. I have had Other Praying Mothers, specifically a little dynamo of a woman in Pearl, Mississippi, by the name of Mrs. (Maizie) James. She has many children and grandchildren of her own, yet chose to adopt me as a daughter-in-prayer and prays for me every single day. She will call me and leave sweet messages on my voice mail like, "I love you and I am so proud of you. I pray for you twice a day, every day." When I am feeling discouraged and tired, sometimes all I have to do is remember that my Other Praying Mother is choosing to cover me.

Other Mothers are a gift we give ourselves and our daughters. To have Other Mothers does not diminish your own mother, and by having them in your life, you are not being emotionally unfaithful to your mother. Author Richard Bach said, "The bond that links your true family is not one of blood, but of respect and joy in each other's life." There is a richness in the many women who can step in and care for us, impart life experience and wisdom to us, and give of themselves to another generation. We are the better for them.

And so are our daughters. I can't see that my mother or I would be the women we are without the lingering influence of Nana in our lives. Nana is the one who taught us about tenacity in tough times and the rewards of faithfulness in the life of a believer and that a meal did not have to be elaborate to be wonderful. So it is that Nana's presence is with us, in my mother and myself, as we look at Elyse and see the generational ripples in the pond.

We have so many women who can come alongside us in our children's lives to bring other perspectives. As wonderful as any mom is, our daughters will still need some Other Mother. And we need not be intimidated or threatened by this, but simply thank God that our daughter is gaining a wealth of voices in her life.

As Elyse's mom I am grateful for an unlikely Other Mother, her sixth grade homeroom teacher. Ms. Julie Jenkins was a kind soul who came alongside Elyse in her first year of middle school. (Elyse did NOT like middle school AT ALL, and Ms. Jenkins took an interest in her.) It was a year after my father passed and our family was trying to learn how to deal with that sort of cataclysmic loss, and Elyse just needed someone else to talk to. Ms. Jenkins saw a gap and filled a gap. The best Other Mothers sometimes just jump in. I can honestly say that I pray for Elyse to have a slew of Other Mothers in her life, women who can fill the gaps I might not even be able to see.

You may be a woman who needs an Other Mother. You might be a woman with Other Mothering to give. Truth is, you're probably both. I hope that you will seek out the Other Mothers you need and give Other Mothering liberally to the girls coming up the path behind you. Maybe, in that case, if it's not one thing, it's your Other.

utter
✳momsense

When you are pregnant you spend lots of time telling yourself that you are NOT going to be like your mother. Even if you have experienced a great relationship with your mom, this sense comes over you that you are going to be The One, The Mother of Proverbs 31 whose children rise up and call her "Blessed!" You are going to be there for them and be the mom who always has ancient wisdom available in relevant vernacular! You are going to keep it fresh for your kids! You aren't going to fall back on those same trite phrases you've heard a thousand times from your mother and everyone else's mom.

And then you hear yourself say it.

You can't quite believe it, but you just said it.

Somewhere around the time your baby gets upwardly mobile and starts with the "But why, Mom?" questions, you utter the words that torpedo your finest intentions to break the Trite Mother Sayings Cycle: "Because I said so, that's why."

And soon thereafter, you join with the Mom Song of the Ages, that river of collective mother wisdom that seems to spout effort-lessly from the mouths of moms, prefaced by (spoken or unspo-ken): "Just let me give you a word of advice . . ." Scientific studies have proven that moms are physically incapable of *not* giving advice if they believe they are in possession of a better way to think, act, or proceed. This is known as Compulsive Counsel Disorder.

I did have a tiny moment of thinking that my mom might have some sage advice when I was six years old. I can't recall the exact details of the incident but someone was treated cruelly on our bus on the way to school. Whatever happened was serious enough that our entire busload of riders got called in to the principal's office. When our principal asked if any of us had anything to say for ourselves I raised my chubby little first-grader hand and spouted off verbatim something my mom had told me just a couple of days before. I said, "We cannot undo what has already been done, but if we ask God to forgive us and try to make things right, we can do better the next time."

My principal looked as though the heavens had opened and the angels had poured, singing, into her office. She nodded her head and asked me to write down what I had just said and bring it back to her office the next day. She framed it and hung it right there on the same wall as her college diploma. It was the only time in my childhood I recall thinking that maybe Mom's advice had something to it, after all. Then the little window of revelation closed, never to open again until I reached about twenty-two.

The little known fact regarding the Mother Code of Wis-dom is that it was DNA encoded with Eve and is impossible to eradicate. And it doesn't matter if you were actually mothered by your own mother. *Some* mother somewhere said these things to you and they were instantly placed into your memory bank for the exact moment when you would need them: when you became a mother yourself.

Here is but an introductory list of these Momsense Gems, as I'm sure you have some of your own to add:

"Bundle up." This could mean any number of things: (1) Your mom has already been outside and knows that it is cold enough to make you sick, or (2) She saw the forecast this morning and thinks it's probably cold outside, or (3) She is cold.

"Make your bed." She wants to know that you are no longer in it and that you won't drop Oreo crumbs on the sheets sometime during the day.

"Clean your room." Impossible to accomplish since moms and kids will never agree on the definition of "clean." Still an important concept as she doesn't want your future roommate or spouse to judge her parental skills based on your lack of tidiness. She also wants you to . . .

"Clean your plate. Lots of children in Third World countries are starving." I call this the Mom's World Hunger Awareness Campaign. If she has a visual aid of a map of the world she can use this teachable moment to show you exactly where the starving children are located. (That would also be a dead giveaway that she is a homeschool mom.) But all Moms know guilt and know how to use it at opportune moments. This is the way she gets you to . . .

"Eat your vegetables." Medical science is actually backing Mom up on this one. What she doesn't seem to remember is that lots of veggies fall under the category of "acquired taste" and have bizarre textures. And is there a baby alive who just flails their widdle arms in joy when Mommy unscrews the lid to the pureed lima beans? If they could make vegetables taste like Twinkies, problem solved.

And while we're on the subject of eating, how about this one that doesn't make sense from the get go: "Close your mouth and eat." Any idea how you could eat without *opening* your mouth?

"A place for everything and everything in its place." Mom normally uses this one when you have committed a flagrant foul of not putting something back that she uses all the time (tape dispenser, electric mixer, Valium). This is not the time to point out that the item *was* in a place, just a *different* place. If you do choose to risk it and she looks at you with the Medusa eye, she might tell you:

"Get that hair out of your eyes." I have to say that this is a personal pet peeve of mine. They say that the eyes are the windows of the soul and, when moms are trying to peer into your soul they really don't want to have to use their x-ray vision to get past the bangs. So we call for the windows of the soul to be available for us to peer into with our emotional x-ray vision. All moms believe that if they can look into your eyes they can know the truth. Which leads us to the next momish saying . . .

"Look at me when I'm talking to you." I've read in magazines that if you are walking or jogging through your neighborhood and encounter a less-than-friendly dog, the absolute worst thing you can do is make eye contact with it. Perhaps this is what kids instinctively do when moms are giving them The What For and they look away. I'm not sure what drives it, but I know for sure that it drives moms up the ever lovin' wall. They want to lock eyes with you, so "get that hair outta your eyes AND look at me when I'm talking to you!" Ooooooo, a double Momsense.

How about one that is just physically impossible: "Would you take a look at this dirt behind your ears?"

Or the one that shows the level of compassion moms have for their children when the wee ones are obviously upset: "Stop crying or I'll give you something to cry about!"

And then there's, "Don't use that tone of voice with me." (Even less sense: "Don't look at me in that tone of voice.") Moms have hair trigger Attitude Radar. They especially get exercised over the issue of verbal disrespect. When moms feel that they are about to be disrespected, the hair actually goes up on the back of their neck. They get all tingly and want to give you fair warning that it doesn't really matter *what* you are about to say since JUST THE TONE OF YOUR VOICE is enough to get you in a heap of trouble. It's like an early warning system so you can know when you're about ten words shy of doing something very stupid. Past this point lie only the skeletons of your former social life. This would be a prudent time to back it down a notch or two.

"Shut that door. Were you born in a barn?" It seems like this is a question that only the mom would know the answer to, but the door-shutting admonition stands. We want the door closed (to save heat, to save air conditioning, to block the noise and save our sanity). But we want it closed properly, which leads us to . . .

"Don't slam that door!" Just close it. And by the way . . .

"Is that what you're going to wear?"

"No, Mom, I'm just doing a science experiment to see which sorts of fibers stay clean longer."

Of course you are wearing that. And if you really want Mom's opinion on what you are wearing, perhaps she should consider taking your temperature instead. It just isn't in the natural order of things.

"Do as I say, not as I do." This is every parent's hope—that our children will do better than we do. It's also our way of admitting that we're not perfect and prefer that you will excuse our moral laziness while we tell you one thing and do another. It is not our finest parental moment, and if we owned one of those Memory Nebulizers from the movie *Men in Black*, we would flash you so that you would not be able to recall our glaring inconsistency. The following classic Momsense illustrates this perfectly: "If I've told you once, I've told you a thousand times—don't exaggerate!"

And then there's: "Just be yourself." This is what moms say when they are encouraging their kids to embrace their authenticity and originality. What moms seem clueless about is that for children of a certain age, to be authentic or original would be the kiss of death. They don't want to stand out, they want to blend in. There will be plenty of time to "be yourself" later, because right now they just desperately want to be someone else. Anyone else. Preferably with someone else's parents.

"Use your own judgment." This is the Great Mother of All Conundrums. What it seems like you're saying is, "You think about this and decide for yourself what is right and then do it." But a more accurate interpretation would be, "You'd better think long and hard about the advice I just gave you. This gem is the result of many, many years of experience as well as the memory of painful consequences I have brought upon myself. Now, I don't want you having to learn the same lessons the hard way. So listen up. If you choose to do something other than the course I have advised you to take, I will *not* be responsible for the outcome. And I will never let you forget it." In other words, "Use *my* judgment."

And that leads me to a final Momsense, which, with all of Mom's compulsive repetition, doesn't make *any* sense: "Don't make me tell you again."

What's amazing is that kids seem impervious to virtually all of these statements. It's as if their underdeveloped ear canals have no way to let the wisdom of these phrases get past the earwax. (This may actually be the cause of all the earaches and ear infections in small children: Wisdom Buildup in the ear canal.) But even though your kids don't seem like they're listening to any of the fine advice you're offering them (FREE OF CHARGE, mind you), something kicks in around the age of twenty-one and all the Momsense you gave them finally crosses the waxy canal to find a resting place in their brains . . . where it lies dormant until they have children of their own to release it upon.

eating
your
young

The many charms of cable TV—more channels, more choices, a veritable banquet of specialized programming and narrowly niched shows. So why is it that we spend our allotted TV time surfing through however-many-channels-your-cable-has just to find that we have the same problem we had when there were four on VHF and two on UHF (for those readers under forty, skip it—it's too hard to explain): There's *still* nothing on that we want to watch! (We can, however, see channels devoted to twenty-four-hour poker, bass fishing, book lectures, knitting, extreme sports, court cases, and makeovers.)

This is another instance of how *more* choices do not make us happier, just more frustrated. "How in the world," we wonder, "could there be so many channels and I can't find something I want to watch?!" Thus you decide that the problem must lie with you and that you must be a channel-surfing loser. In your weakened, intimidated state you give up on anything entertaining and resign yourself to watching things that seem educational. And, let's face it, there's only so much C-SPAN one can watch before you decide that all elected officials are verbose camera hogs. That leads to more surfing for an acceptable educational alternative, which is how most people get started watching the Discovery Channel, Animal Planet, or National Geographic TV. These are the airwaves that fill your evenings with hollowed-out zebra carcasses, elephant mating rituals, and crazy people collecting snake venom. Mmmm, great relaxing programming.

If you watch the Animal Planet for more than thirty minutes you notice that, in the animal kingdom, there are multiple mothering styles. You've got your marsupials who carry their young in their pouch for a while; the mares with their colts who let their babies run alongside them and try to keep up. There are the mom cats who, once they have a litter of kitties, evenly divide their time between giving milk and giving tongue baths. Mama Ducks march in front and expect their baby ducklings to waddle in line behind. Mama Bear is legendary for her protective nature. Most animal experts agree that one of the most dangerous places on earth for a human to be is between a mama bear and her cub.

I did find it fascinating to learn that mama eagles anticipate their babies leaving the nest even while they are building it. The mama eagle adds sharp and jagged objects toward the bottom of the nest before they line it with soft things so that as the baby eaglet gets larger and starts wearing away the soft lining, it is met with things that make the nest gradually more and more uncomfortable. This is so the baby will *want* to leave. Perhaps this is why the eagle is our national symbol—we admire the way they encourage their adolescents to leave the nest.

Other little known mom facts you can learn from watching animal channels: Polar bears sleep through labor (I wonder what's in their epidural!), and elephants give birth to 200 pound "babies" (give that elephant mom whatever the polar bear is having).

In the movie *March of the Penguins* we were afforded a cinematic window into the mating and mothering of the waddling mass of tuxedoed birdfish. They pair off—although I didn't get a clear understanding of the criteria for choice ("Oh, you have black and white on your body. Nice. And your eyes are black and round. That's what I like about you, you're not like all the others."). They stand around a while (I don't know if there is more to it than that, but if there is, the movie didn't show it) and then wait for the egg to drop (literally). One day the mom lifts her furry "skirt" and shows the daddy penguin the egg. She carefully rolls it over the ice to Dad, and he takes charge for several weeks while all the moms march seventy miles for a meal. (If I had to waddle that far over frozen tundra to get to the next meal you could just go ahead and dig the hole for my burial.) The dads do The Egg Hatch Huddle for a couple of months as the baby penguins chip their way out of the egg only to find—surprise!—baby, it's cold outside! And right at the moment when the babies are about to starve, the Mom Cavalry arrives back from the seafood buffet. Mom regurgitates food for the chick. Yum. Then the mom and dad coo with each other for about a minute, the dad memorizes the chick's warble, and then he says, "Honey, you know I'd love to stick around for the first day of preschool, but I gotta get to the coast before I lose my very last emergency layer of fat."

Penguins are so cute, but they might need to check with MapQuest to see if there might be a chunk of ice closer to the food source to cut back on that killer commute time, eh?

One of the most intriguing studies in mom behavior is that of the praying mantis. These creatures will eat their spouse after they mate and often cannot distinguish between their offspring and their prey (this is an unfortunate tendency in many families), so sometimes they eat their own offspring. Any mother with hormonal issues can see how this might be possible.

When we were growing up we all heard the phrase, "Just wait 'til you have kids of your own." This thinly veiled threat, designed to serve as both a warning and a non explanation of whatever it was we were questioning, always left me wondering what sort of magical lightbulb would illuminate my brain upon having a child of my own—and what might become apparent only at that very moment. I remember thinking as I held my baby in my arms, "*Ah, they must be talking about the love and awesome responsibility you feel when you gaze into this angel's face and know that you are entrusted with this sweet gift.*" But you only get the full effect of that phrase when your kids celebrate birthday thirteen.

When you have teenagers in your house you start to think the Praying Mantis Mom Thoughts. Others must have thought them, too, as these are actual headlines that appeared in newspapers: *Include Your Children When Baking Cookies* and *Kids Make Nutritious Snacks.*

In some cruel scripting of hormonal ironies it is often the case that moms are entering into peri- or full-blown menopause about the same time that their daughters are requiring feminine protection. Could this be a good plan? That the temperamental mood swings of the mother are coinciding with the hormonal angst of her adolescent daughter? Not to mention that it is common knowledge that females who live or work in the same proximity eventually begin cycling together. And not on bikes.

One thing that is particularly annoying to moms of teenagers nowadays is how they are "aware" enough to call us on our own inconsistencies. We all know how much we love *that*. My friend Stacy had a talk with her daughter concerning her overuse of The Eyeroll whenever she was being talked to. Stacy explained how rude and disrespectful it was and that it was a bad habit that needed to stop. Her daughter agreed to try to do better. Within a week of this conversation Stacy's mom came for a visit, and when she left, Stacy's daughter said, "Mom, you can never talk to me again about me rolling my eyes because you rolled *your* eyes about a million times while Grandma was here."

Stacy told me that the only thing that flashed through her mind in that moment was, "I am so *busted*!" This is mainly because when your daughter is a teenager she turns into one large hypocrisy antennae, and her main purpose in life is to spot any contradictions between what you say and what you do. It is highly upsetting to find out that your children have actually listened to all your lectures on morality and now have the vocabulary to call you out on it.

If you are a mother of a teenage daughter be assured that the hormones (and maybe even the judgments) will probably dein-tensify about the time she leaves for college or her first adult job. Meanwhile, I can give you a couple of my favorite mom-of-teenager tricks to help see you through.

When my kids were all teenagers (yes, *at the same time*) I had just about had it with droning the incessant reminder to put their napkins in their laps before they started to eat their meal. So I made a rule (all good moms know how to make spontaneous rules) that if you took a single bite of food before your napkin was in your lap you had to go to another room of the house and sing "The Star Spangled Banner" loudly enough to be heard at the dinner table. May I just say that at least one of my children is truly prepared should Major League Baseball call for a singer. And what a mom I am—instilling a sense of patriotism AND good manners with one fell swoop.

Here's another good one: If you are the one footing the cell phone bill for your teenagers and you are tired of them not responding when *you* ring them up, you can borrow our "Three Strikes and You're Out" rule. This means that we (the loving parents) can call you one time and believe that you could be temporarily out of range or in a place where it's difficult to hear the phone. And if we call you a second time, we might be able to believe that you might still have an issue of coverage or ringtone volume. But, baby, if we call you a third time and you are not picking up that cell, we will know that you are screening your bill-paying source and will repossess your technological umbilical cord until you are able to pay your bill yourself. Love can be tough sometimes.

So when you are being challenged by your teenage daughter about your inconsistencies or explaining for the forty-fourth time why she needs to listen to your wisdom, you might have a couple of fleeting Praying-Mantis-Mom thoughts of your own. I have found that it is helpful to get out the cute toddler pictures at this point to reidentify these adolescent creatures as your offspring. And if you keep your own private stash of chocolate you won't be as tempted to eat your young.

the land mine
of all
holidays

This is why America is a great nation: We have a Sunday in May dedicated to the proposition that mothers are worthy of flowery cards, candy, and a meal in a restaurant and another Sunday in June that proclaims that dads are worthy of . . . um . . . well, either some grill tools or another necktie.

You can see this uneven devotion to mothers even when you are watching sporting events on TV. You will notice that invariably the athletes mouth the words, "Hi Mom!" from the sidelines when the cameras are turned on them or after any great play. This is because they know that, if they are on TV, Mama's watchin'. Her eyes are glued on them from the time the game came on until the bitter or victorious end. One cannot say the same of Dad. Most of the time Dad is in and out of the TV room getting snacks, going to the bathroom, trying to find the remote, or fiddling around with the TiVo or VCR. So kids know which gender to address on national TV. They know that it will do a mama good to be acknowledged in front of the masses and that this public display of affection can wipe out many offenses. Not that moms keep up with those as a rule, but we do have a little mental tally running on the things we do or don't get on Mother's Day.

I remember Mother's Day 1983. John and I had been married nine months and I was three months pregnant. We went to church that morning and the pastor asked all the mothers or mothers-to-be to stand so we could be honored and the ushers handed out red roses to each mom. It was my first time to stand with the motherly ones. I felt like I had just been inducted into some secret society. Little did I know that this honoring of Mother's Day—celebrated for years in some other countries—had some difficulty coming together here in the U. S. of A.

Apparently Mother's Day started as two separate attempts to bring attention to the plights of American moms. When an Appalachian woman organized a day to bring awareness of how poor the health conditions were in her area, Anna Jarvis named the day "Mother's Work Day" (which, in my opinion, was bizarre and redundant, as any mother would tell you that this would describe pretty much *every* day after she's had a child). In the same decade, Julia Ward Howe (the author of the lyrics to "The Battle Hymn of the Republic" and, interestingly enough, not a mother—which explains why she had the energy to write stirring songs and dream up new national holidays) was organizing some sort of national recognition for the mothers who had suffered devastating losses due to the Civil War. When Anna Jarvis died in 1905, her daughter (also named Anna) took up the torch for her cause and organized Mother's Friendship Days in 1907. It caught on in her state of West Virginia and eventually was declared a national holiday by President Woodrow Wilson in 1914. Thus the second Sunday in May became Mother's Day.

The million dollar question when it comes time to pay homage to dear old Mom (just don't call her that to her face) is, "What *does* Mom want for Mother's Day?"

The answer: No such wish list exists.

The problem: Moms are so different. Yet, amazingly, the same.

See, we all really want something that conveys how our child feels about us. This explains the proliferation of the flowery, swirly, overly decorated greeting cards. Nowhere in the publishing or gift world are there so many flourishes used than in the Mother's Day time frame. It seems that either we feel elaborately toward our mothers or at least we want them to *think* that's how we feel about them. And nothing says "I think you're the best mom ever" than a card that says it <u>and</u> has the words underlined and decorated with massive swirling curly cues. It's almost like we're overly emphatic, hoping that the curvy lines will distract her from the fact that we haven't called in six weeks.

Moms also want something that shows that you care for us. This explains the candy, the flowers, and the taking out to dinner. The candy says, "You're not fat. You can afford the extra calories." The flowers say, "You're special and thank goodness the grocery store had this last bouquet in stock because I didn't pick it up until the trip over." The dinner out says, "It's your special day! Don't cook! Let's pay someone to do the thing we let you do for free all these years!"

These things are well and good, but mothers also want something that says, "I know what it is that you like and what makes you unique," which is why all the flourish-heavy cards, flowers, candy, and eating out just won't cut it. Oh, moms will act all happy if that's all you come up with. A Good Mom will never tell you she is disappointed that you didn't do something more original. She will just smile and kiss you before you take off on Mother's Day night, and as you are pulling out of the driveway, she will think (fondly, of course), "*That was lame.*"

I have given some less-than-stellar gifts to my own mom in years past. I can recall one really great pecan sheller I gave her in 1987 (it sounds dumb, but you'd have to understand how much she loves pecans). It looked a little bit like a mounted slingshot that used the tension from a rubber band to pop the pecan open. The demonstration made it look simple and effective, but in reality it smashed the pecans to smithereens and left a whole lotta shell pummeled into the pecan meat. I wouldn't want to analyze that gift in Freudian terms.

My husband did a good job of helping our children learn the Mother's Day ropes. It was so cute when they were little and he would take them to the store to purchase items for my Mother's Day Breakfast Tray. This tradition was carefully executed from year to year and accompanied by precious handmade cards. But since Mother's Day is always on a Sunday and I was a minister's wife, I had no time to enjoy it. Any pastor's wife can tell you that the Lionel Richie "Easy Like Sunday Morning" lyric is just a lie. But on my tray I would get fresh fruit and whipped cream, juice and coffee, a nice pastry, and a gift from John (for being his kids' mother), along with something from each child. I remember the year that Austin wrapped up his favorite Teenage Mutant Ninja Turtle in a sock. That was a gift of pure love.

They say that the hand that rocks the cradle rules the world. But I ask you—how great a job of ruling the world is Mom gonna do if she has only had three hours of uninterrupted sleep at a time? If this sleep-deprived woman is ruling the world we might stop holding our breath for world peace. So I would suggest that the thing new moms need most is a Mother's Day Nap. In fact, if you want to really go over the top, give her a Mother's Day Weekend Nap package—which would include the entire family evacuating the premises for four hours each day so that Mom could take a hot bath, climb into bed without hearing ANY NOISES COMING FROM ANYWHERE, and sleep for three uninterrupted hours that aren't between 1 and 4 AM. If you did that for three days in a row (Friday, Saturday, and Sunday), it could reboot her sleep system and you might just encounter a deliriously happy woman.

I can tell you that Mom does *not* want anything that plugs into the wall (unless it's a new Jacuzzi—that would be an exception). Anything that reminds her of cooking and cleaning you can toss, too. The fact is, anything you could bring to her would merely be a token of what you feel for her, but if you value your life, DON'T SKIP THE TOKEN.

What do moms want on this day when you could really mess up and then suffer the consequences for some time to come? I can offer a few suggestions, but it varies from mom to mom.

If you've got some extra cash on ya—

- A cleaning person once a month for a year (after she picked up HOW MANY of your socks?)
- A day at a spa once a month (she rocked, soothed, and patted you to sleep a few thousand times, so it's time to return the favor—and just imagine the good thoughts coming your way each time she goes for that ultimate relaxation)
- Tickets to Hawaii (send your mom someplace that will make her friends jealous—she'll sing your praises for years, *plus* it will really make your siblings look cheap! Two birds!)

For the less extravagant—

- You think up the meal, you buy for the meal, you fix the meal, you clean up the meal. (Mom wants to see your EFFORT!)
- Four new bath products and three protected hours to use them. (If you set up a fruit and cheese tray ahead of time, you are really racking up the points.)

For the flat out broke—

- Get with your siblings and sign a binding contract that says you will choose to be nice to each other at all family functions for the next five years. Get it notarized. I guarantee it will make her unbelievably happy for only about five bucks.

- If you are an only child, it is the best of times and the worst of times. Best because you have no other sibling's present for her to compare, worst because all the pressure is on you. If you are an only and you are broke, go for the pen and paper and write something truly heartfelt and wonderful. Moms always love a good letter.

In fact, no matter what your birth order or financial status, you may want to break out the crayons for a construction paper card—hey, it worked in third grade, didn't it? You may need to borrow lines from *The Waltons*. Whatever works. What is Mother's Day without a mushy card? Believe me—you don't want to find out.

smotherly
❋ love

When you are a baby it is comforting.

When you are a kid it seems annoying.

When you are a teenager you think you will die of it.

When you are an adult it seems insulting.

It is the difficulty mothers have judging distance between themselves and their child. If they are going to err it's almost always on the side of too close. This is a problem that's almost all tied into emotions and geography. Kids start off as close as they can possibly be — inside of us. All it takes for either mom or daughter to acknowledge this intimate connection is a glance at the little wrinkly divet in the middle of our middles (or, for some of you "outies" a little bump in the belly landscape). Belly buttons remind us that we came from somewhere, some*one*, and that we were not hatched, we were attached. Our physical detachment is marked by this funny little belly button, but we all have to gradually detach emotionally from the Maternal Unit.

You can talk about being Daddy's Girl all you want, but whether the chips are down or the gloves are off, moms and daughters are attached. Sometimes it's like two polecats with their tails tied tossed over a clothesline, but we are attached. We are the girls of the house, bound by gender, cosmetics, hair issues, and hormones.

Once our daughters move outside of us we have a little separation, but we still keep them very near to us night and day. Then they start crawling and they start moving away from us, and we still keep them in our sights. Then they start walking and it starts with the walking toward us so that they can fall into our arms, but it eventually leads to walking away from us. We are taught by experience that things happen when they are away from us that cause them to run back to us requiring first aid. This makes us nervous. Then a school bus takes them away for part of the day. Then the driver's license allows them to go farther. Then it's time to move away, and a mom's heart has never really gotten past the fact that you crawled away all those years ago.

Let's get real — moms would like to hang on to their job. It has been one defining aspect of our life for a good while. If we have been looking out for your well-being for double digits you have to admit that instinct might be a little difficult to turn off without some fits and starts and sputters. We don't really want our children tied to our apron strings, but if they could just hang on by a leeetle thread that wouldn't be so terrible, would it?

All of this makes for some difficult navigations through the "series of gradually harder good-byes." It's not that moms set out to smother you, it's just that they don't really know how to stop. It is hard to develop healthy emotional distance from someone when you were her Womb Raider for the first months of your existence. And when you surfaced this woman was your caretaker and guardian. She lived in her own version of the movie *Groundhog Day* during your toddler years and answered your kajillion questions as you came into early childhood. Your mom served as your moral compass, Jiminy Cricket, and Impossible Rule Maker when you were a teen and helped you chart out a plan to create independence as a young adult. So why is it so hard to understand why she has a difficult time letting go? It is safe to say that the woman who changed your millionth diaper and rode with you when you had your learner's permit is probably going to have a hard time seeing you as fully adult.

But daughters feel a powerful drive to separate to autonomy and can't wait to fire their emotional rocket boosters and achieve their own adult orbit. For some this happens earlier in their teens and causes a good bit of drama as the timetables for finishing school and financial independence don't always sync up with their feelings of restlessness.

I remember being so conflicted as a teenage daughter. I knew that I wasn't quite grown yet but I wanted to be so badly. It's like you are spending all your time on the launching pad and you are just itching for the NASA countdown. I see it in my own daughter. She sometimes feels restless and unsettled. She loves being the princess here at home but knows that season is winding down for her. It is bittersweet and a time of inner conflict for mothers and daughters, this letting out of the emotional lifeline.

And daughters may feel anxious about revealing their personal changes to us and wonder how we will respond. My friend Ellie relates a funny story about such an instance with her daughter.

Paris came home on Thanksgiving weekend for her fresh-man year break. She shared late Thursday night that she really needed to talk to me and that it was important. The weekend got busy with food and friends and visits and she insisted Sunday morning that we absolutely needed to talk. I saw the intensity in her eyes and took her inside a locked room. I grabbed both hands and locked eyes and urged her to share and apologized for making her wait three days.

Her eyes finally settled on mine after looking away a few times.

"What is it, baby? What's troubling you?"

"Mom . . . Mom . . . I'm . . . I'm . . . Mom, I'm not a Republican anymore!"

I held her close and breathed a deep sigh.

"Don't you worry—we'll love you no matter what, and we'll work it out."

And, as daughters, we can become living embodiments of the Elvis song, "Suspicious Minds." We think that our mom wants to know everything about us just so she can continue to direct our lives with this knowledge (for some this may be true, but it's prob-ably the exception). Mothers are the people who find every minute detail of their daughter's life interesting. Daughters are the people who find this trait almost impossible to appreciate.

This has been a difficult issue for my mom and me because of my mom's particular gifts. She loves to make home an inviting, warm, hospitable place to be and has been an integral part of our ability to have a ministry that is sometimes away from home for the last several years. That meant that, because she lives with us, her knowledge of our life was far more extensive than if she lived in another town or another state. I remember the day I totally went off on my mom because this came to a head. I was feeling resentful because of all the things she was privy to. She has super-sensitive hearing for water running so she literally knows every time someone turns on a faucet or if the toilet handle sticks in our house. And every phone call that comes in. And every piece of mail that comes in and every person that comes to the door and every time I go to the mall and every time I have a cold. It's not that she *shouldn't* know that stuff, it's just not *normal* for her to know it without my telling her. That's really just too much knowledge for anyone other than your spouse. And normally even *he* doesn't know all that. As thankful as I was for my mom's presence in our home so that we could travel and minister part of the time, it was a time to ask for some voluntary boundaries.

This is difficult for mothers and daughters. When I would feel it was time to discuss this with my mom I would literally put it off for weeks because I knew she would view it as ungrateful on my part. When daughters ask for space it's hard for a mom to believe that it's not driven by disloyalty or selfishness. But I can say from my own experience that it is essential to feel that your life is your own. As much as you love your mother and want to have an intimate lifelong relationship with her, there are portions of your life that must be separate to be healthy. The amount of emotional space it takes to have a feeling of adult-ness and autonomy will vary from relationship to relationship. But from time to time, new boundaries will have to be set up and honored.

In my situation, because my mom lives here, we have found that it's necessary to decide what is important to each female and figure out our preferences and nonnegotiables. It is important to identify them and to talk with your mother about them. For my mom, she loves, loves, LOVES to do laundry. She will go around the house and solicit different kinds of clothes for loads she is "getting up" (this is a concept that makes perfect sense to her, but I cannot understand why anyone would want to "get up" a load). This turns into a game of Laundry Go Fish.

"Anybody got any darks?"

"No, Mom. I've got a delicate and a towel but no darks. Go fish."

She does loads of laundry pretty much every day and enjoys it immensely. I would only do laundry if no one in our house had clean underwear *and* Target was closed so that we couldn't buy any. Just how stupid it would be of me to insist that she let me do laundry two days a week just so I could make a point about having some ownership of the laundry room. I know that's not important to me. I know that it's important to her. She can have it.

By the same token, my mom agonizes over making large purchases. She will look and look and look for curtains or furniture, she will decide and then second guess her decisions. She will bring stuff home and take it back several times before she decides that she doesn't like any of it. Not me. I can sweep through a store and make decisions in a single day and feel confident that I got the right thing and enjoy it. This doesn't stress me in the least. How foolish it would be of her to insist that she go with me to make large purchases for our home? A willingness to give and take and the self-knowledge to discern what is important goes a long way toward peaceful coexistence.

I realize that most of the mothers and daughters reading this do not have our living arrangements, but the principles are the same. When your mom comes to visit you can have the same sort of feeling of encroachment if you haven't figured out what is truly important to you and what areas you could just allow your mom to be free in. Everything is not important. Not every hill is worth dying on. Some areas aren't your forte and it doesn't really matter to you one way or the other. Is there some place we could meet and live in harmony there?

One problem we have between mothers and daughters is that we haven't fully thought about what we need. I think we need gullies. Gullies are usually created by rain.

My mom and my daughter both love rain. They love it for different reasons, but their response to rain is much the same. My mom is a farmer's daughter and will actually clap her hands like a child on Christmas morning when she hears the rain start to fall on our skylights in the kitchen. She will watch the Weather Channel just so she can see the patterns of clouds passing over us,

around us, south or north of us. When we call in from another
state to check in she will tell us, "There was a little cloud right over
us, and it looked like we were going to get a little something, but
it passed us by and we got nothing. Not even a drop."

My daughter loves rain because she thinks dark days are the
best. She is an indoors chick and the rain means she will be inside
all day. Plus she likes to nap and cloudy days are just conducive to
great napping. In this way I am sure that I had some genetic influence in her life, even though I am an all-weather napper.

But rain is what makes gullies—actually it's the runoff from
the rain. It's not as large as a stream or a river, just an oversized
ditch that separates two pieces of land and allows the excess rain
to run off and not damage the structures on either side. When I
think of what I want with my mom and what I believe my daughter will want as an adult with me, I think of a gully. It's nicely
formed with enough distance for distinct separation but not so
much that you can't jump across should a situation warrant it. It's
also a place where excess emotion can run off from conversations
and situations without damaging either of us permanently.

There are times when we react to situations and use an emotional
nuclear device to create something that is an unmeasured response.
We drop a "bomb" to display our need for space and end up with
a divide that is too wide to get across and stand on the other side
wondering what happened—we now have a Grand Canyon instead
of a gully. Then there comes a time when we desperately need the
affection and comfort that only our mom can give us, but we have
left no way to cross over. The span is just too wide.

I think it falls to the grown daughter to consider the distance of the division you need between yourself and your mom. Given the way the relationship starts out, it is easy to see how the idea of separation is so much more difficult for the mom than for the daughter. Daughters' lives are about carving out more autonomy and freedom. As a rule, mothers' lives are spent grieving and adjusting to whatever new level their girl is creating. As much as your mom wants you to live your own life, she would still like to be included more than you would probably feel comfortable allowing. It is hard to make gullies instead of canyons when you are reacting to the feeling that your life needs wider emotional margins of separation.

If a mother and daughter have a strong relationship and both try to follow biblical principles the theory is that this whole negotiation should be easier, but I'm not sure it is. We need shovelfuls of self-respect and courage to get the gullies started, walls of love and mutual respect to keep them from becoming too large, the emotional rains to wash them out and keep them clean and free-flowing, and the connection that comes from inviting each other to jump the gully every now and again.

If only we could make a temporary perspective shift where we could somehow get into each other's brain for a few minutes, we would be able to see that the smotherly love is not meant to infringe and the daughterly need for boundaries isn't meant to shut out. The ties that bind us are enduring, endearing, and just a little bit maddening. C'est la vie femme. Viva la différence!

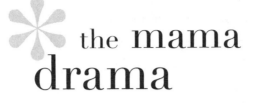

the mama drama

In the theater world it happens regularly—shows are floated up to Broadway after someone has worked years trying to open there. There are high hopes for good reviews and ticket sales. The show opens, the show fails, the show folds. The elusive Long Run on Broadway is a rarity, indeed. The shows that dramatically connect with an audience in such a way that people keep coming year after year after year are a statistical anomaly. And there are some that just don't go away, such as . . .

The Phantom of the Opera (my husband's personal favorite, although for the life of me I have no idea why). We saw it at the Kennedy Center in Washington DC years ago and he has been a big fan ever since. I think it might be the rock and roll power chords played on a pipe organ—analyze that!

Cats (never seen it, but I hear it's the pick of the litter. Ba da bing! Rimshot, please!)

Les Misérables (apparently about airplane passengers trapped on a commuter flight with six teething babies).

In the mother/daughter relationship, theatrics seem to come with the territory—no stage training required. We can ratchet up the drama to the brink of annihilation and are not afraid to initiate a full-scale meltdown every now and then should the situation warrant it. Moms can crank up the drama to produce their desired results. Daughters can flail about, roll their eyes, slam doors, and huff around to show how their mom is, in fact, ruining their life. Both sides know how to make their point and then drive it home with the perfect just-over-the-top amount of histrionics. It's hard to put the brakes on when we have been in this longest running production, The Mama Drama, far longer than *Phantom* or *Cats*.

Coming from The South I can tell you that Southern women excel in their flair for Mother/Daughter Tony Award-Worthy performances. If you watch any depiction of Southern life and there are mothers and daughters in the script there will be sparks and conflicts and storming off and apologies and crying jags and sinking spells and hissy fits. We Southern women are not given to emotional temperance. We believe that is best left to steady Midwesterners, reserved Northerners, or laid-back West Coasters. I do realize that there are women of those regions who can hold their own in the drama department, but as a rule those women only occasionally participate in the type of behaviors that Southern women perpetually cultivate. Think *Steel Magnolias* and *Ya Ya Sisterhood*.

If we need a pause in the conflict, we can develop a sudden case of "the vapors." No one can actually give a medical definition of "the vapors," but we know that it causes us to swoon, temporarily lose focus, cause someone to get us a glass of iced water (better yet, sweet tea), and gives us time to collect our thoughts and garner sympathy before we proceed. "The vapors" is virtually uncontestable, as no one knows exactly what it is.

A full-on "hissy fit" is a state that a woman throws herself into completely. It doesn't matter what the precipitating conflict may be, when a woman goes into Hissy Mode you might as well give up any thoughts of reasoning with her. She is now given over completely to emotion and no amount of logic may be applied whatsoever. And note that we always *throw* a hissy fit. Like it is something hurled out from us. Actually, that's pretty accurate. When you are "throwing" one you are definitely putting EVERYTHING you are feeling out there for all the world to see. Men hate to see a woman who is throwing one but other women find it somewhat amusing to watch. Hissy fits don't normally last long as they take a great deal of energy to keep their momentum going.

A "sinking spell" is different from "the vapors" as you may actually go limp and lose vision for a couple of seconds. It is less than a "faint" but more than a "vapor." My grandmother used to have sinking spells at strategic times (like if she was finding out that someone was pregnant for the fifth time or just got a tattoo, or both). I always hypothesized that these sinking spells were low blood sugar in an emotional wrapper, but as I get older I know that certain pieces of information can make you go all weak to where you just need to sit down for a minute.

I offer you this much-detailed definition about the various Mama performances only because, should you find yourself in a situation where you need to use one of these dramatic devices, I know you'll want to employ an appropriate response.

We tend to cross over from the Discussion Mode to the Drama Mode when we perceive that our point of view is either wrong (and we're not willing to change it) or that our perspective is not finding an open mind on the other side of the conversation (and we now must make our point more pointedly). When it gets to this stage mothers are not above making mention of intense, long labor, the dangers of childbirth, and permanent stretch marks, and daughters are not above dragging up a list they keep on record for just such a moment called "The Unforgiveables."

Everyone keeps this list tucked away in the back of her mind. It is a little running tab of some bad things that impacted you greatly at the time they happened. Now, the sting of the event may have faded as the years have passed and you may have honestly forgiven the other person for what they did to you. But forgotten? Not really. Even though the items on our list were rarely life threatening at the time, we still keep them handy for some future argument when we might need to gain a little ground.

I know that on my daughter's list there would be at least two recent entries: I was out of town ON THE DAY of her sixteenth birthday (never mind that we celebrated it for a whole month, I was gone on THE DAY). Also, I sorta kinda ruined the autograph of her favorite hockey player. I mean, who knew that the clear fingernail polish I was putting on the signature he scrawled on her cell phone *in order to preserve it for all time* was actually the only chemical known to mankind that dissolves Sharpie Marker? (Andy Sutton, if you ever hear of this, help a mama get one unforgiveable off the list.) And I may have a little list going with Elyse as well. I have *not* forgotten the day (I think she was about nine years old) when she came into the bathroom, took one look at my pj'd body and stated, "Wow, Mom. I totally get why you wear a bra."

So why *do* we make such a big whoppin' deal about things? Could it be that as moms who are taking care of kids and as daughters who are taking care of moms we get so wrapped up in doing everything to keep everybody floating that we forget the airplane rule? You know the one, ". . . in the event of an emergency — oxygen masks will drop from the ceiling overhead (*help is always available*). Oxygen will be flowing even if the bag does not inflate (*help is there — just out of sight*). Please place the mask over your own nose and mouth before attempting to assist others (*you have to be alive to help someone else*)."

It can be quite revealing to pay attention to the things that set us off into our dramatic performances. If we could get a video of ourselves in those moments I doubt that we would be proud of our behavior. But the question is, "Why do I get so upset about *that?*"

Let's keep it real here — sometimes daughters will use a machine gun to kill a gnat. There are small things that bother us, but instead of addressing the small things along the way, we stuff the minor frustrations until they back up on us. Then we pull out the full ammo clip from the emotional closet and use it to mow her down Terminator-style when the situation only warranted a simple, honest exchange. We say that we are over-emotional because we care, but it's possible that going off does little more than command center stage for a moment. It may not have any real effect on the situation we are trying to change. And with the drama inevitably comes the need to apologize for things we shouldn't have said, expressed in ways we shouldn't have let ourselves express them.

I have heard it said that trying to make your point by throwing a fit is like trying to steer your car by honking the horn. I wonder who among us would be brave enough to go to a trophy store, purchase a statue with "Best Mama Drama" engraved on the base, and tell our children, "I give you permission to hand this to me at any time that I'm on a roll." How many times a day would we need to pull out an acceptance speech?

So how do we choose self-control in those moments when an upsetting subject is on the table for discussion? In Paul's letter to the church at Ephesus we read that we don't have to continue in the old patterns. We can interrupt the well-established cycles and replace them with different responses.

"Stop being mean, bad tempered, and angry," Paul writes. "Quarreling, harsh words, and dislike of others should have no place in your lives. Instead, be kind to each other, tenderhearted, forgiving one another, just as God has forgiven you because you belong to Christ" (Ephesians 5:1-3, 4, TLB).

Paul just puts it out there, and says, "Stop it!" Stop the meanness. Stop choosing to be bad tempered, stop inferring that all your anger is someone else's fault. (We can actually go through life expecting everyone else to change and never look at ourselves.) Stop the quarreling. Stop using harsh words and disliking people just because they are unlike you. Instead substitute kindness and tenderness and forgiveness. Why? Because you aren't that loveable, either, and God chose to forgive you through the sacrifice of His Son, Jesus.

Okay, so it's an understatement to say that we as moms and daughters can push each other's buttons like no one else. And this can be relatively harmless and even humorous—or so potentially damaging that careless words and actions can start a civil war. In the "humorous" vein, it's an occupational hazard with me. I tend to make fun of almost everything—and my mom used to take it ALL personally. To her credit she has learned to laugh at herself too—and now doesn't get offended when we talk about her idiosyncrasies in front of her. Fortunately, my mom and I really don't "fight"—in the sense that there is this huge disconnect over fundamental things. We occasionally "spat," but it is usually over something trivial (she didn't like the way I said something to her; we disagree on whether the important thing is that the cleaning lady gets the hair up off the bathroom floor—my priority—or shines the kitchen cabinets—her priority). And while Elyse can have her "you're-totally-lame-and-I-can't-believe-that-we-share-DNA" eyerolls, we can count on just a few fingers the times we have raised our voices in anger at each other. Elyse and I and Mom and I are learning to appropriately value peace—and to remember what the alternative is when we're picking our battles. Like, if we're going to start World War III it had better be over something that's worth it because we're going to be interacting with each other for the rest of our lives. Keeping peace has taken stretching and giving grace and biting our tongues (pretty much in equal parts).

Next time a Drama Scene unfolds in your house and you are the one up for a Tony nomination, try a different line: Be the first to ask forgiveness. Drama drives us apart. Divine forgiveness brings us close.

"So, chosen by God for this new life of love, dress in the wardrobe God picked out for you: compassion, kindness, humility, quiet strength, discipline. Be even-tempered, content with second place, quick to forgive an offense. Forgive as quickly and completely as the Master forgave you. And regardless of what else you put on, wear love. It's your basic, all-purpose garment. Never be without it" (Colossians 3:12-13).

mental
✳ acreage

My daughter likes to play Monopoly. When she has a few of her friends over for a sleepover they will usually break out the Monopoly board for a game that goes into the wee hours while they discuss the larger issues of life (who's cute, who's not, the latest scoop on what's in and what's out, you know — important stuff). They will play into the wee hours of the morning or until someone is broke. Then they count the money and see who is the Mogul de Jour.

They love it. I don't. I've never really gotten into it. I just don't *get* it. Perhaps it's because I don't know anyone who is in commercial real estate, so it's hard for me to equate anything that happens on the board to anything that happens in real life. I don't get why you have those little die-cast aluminum figurines to go around the board or why you need a "get out of jail free" card. (Why are you *in* jail? What crime did you commit? It seems like you would know if you had committed an ethics violation in your business deals, right?) I don't understand the concept of "community chest" or why people have to pay rent just for landing on your space. I've never known if I should trust whoever is the assigned "banker," because they are over there making change right and left and, frankly, I never know if I got all the right bills back. That part slightly resembles reality.

But I do know that the most important aspect of realty is the same important aspect of body fat: location, location, location. Which means that some real estate on the board is worth a lot more money that some of the others. "Boardwalk" and "Park Place" — now those are the properties you want to snap up early in the game. I personally believe that, after the Boardwalk and Park Place properties are purchased you could just stop the game right there because it's a foregone conclusion that whoever has those is a shoe-in to win.

In the realm of mothers and daughters, we might think of our brain space as a Monopoly board. The figurines are of people who are players in our lives. These people own certain mental properties in our brains and they develop their real estate over the course of our lifetime. Because their influence is first and is lengthy, moms pretty much always end up with Boardwalk and Park Place and have erected massive apartment complexes, condominiums, and other high-rent district buildings across the landscape of our lives. You can't buy 'em out, condemn the property, or evict them. It's their acreage.

When my kids were coming up I had several "speeches" I would give them (every mother does, don't even try to deny it). One that got repeated at predictable intervals was the one I would give them before any of them would leave the house for any length of time (it would have to be for more than a couple of hours—like a sleepover or a youth ski trip or summer camp—something like that). In this classic speech I would remind them of several things—to respect those in authority over them, show Christlike kindness and leadership, stay with a buddy at all times, honor the members of the opposite sex as they would wish someone would treat their sibling, and remember that when they leave the house they are representing the Renfroe name and the family of God. It was short and covered almost every eventuality without a lot of boring details.

After several years of getting The Speech, it got to the point where the kids could recite it verbatim and often I would ask them, "Do you want me to give The Speech or do you want to tell it to me instead?" I figured that if they could spit it back to me then that would just further substantiate that they knew all the provisions they were responsible for. Sure enough, they could tell it to me word for word and I was satisfied that they knew it well. Mental acreage accrued.

Before Austin went to college I was having one of my talks with him about the responsibilities that were stretching out before him and the incredible number of things he would have to prioritize on a daily basis. He said, "Mom, you don't have to worry about this. You don't know it but you already live in my head."

I didn't know whether to rejoice that my voice was firmly established in his decision-making grid or to offer him the name of a good therapist.

You might think you have a choice about it, but some of the

Mom Real Estate Stuff is just pure chemicals. There is a scientific term called "michrochimerism" (I'm not making this up, you can go Google it) whereby, during pregnancy, foreign cells transfer between the mother and the baby (wonder what the exchange rate is?) so that each of you has a portion of the other in you. The child receives some from the mother and the mother receives some from the child. If you are inextricably bound with Mom at the cellular level, then you have little choice over the mental acreage she occupies in your head.

One of my friends' mothers was out shopping for a dress to wear to her mother's 100th birthday. So get the picture here — my friend (in her thirties) was out shopping with her mother (in her early sixties) for a dress to wear to her mother's birthday party — 100-years-old. So the mom comes out of the dressing room in a mighty cute dress. My friend says to her mom, "Wow, Mom! That dress looks great on you — you've just got to get that one!" The mother replies, "Oh, I could never get this one. My mom would never approve."

I could not believe it when my friend told me this story. I thought to myself, *"When does it ever end? When do we ever stop being concerned with Mom's approval?"*

I have a theory that, just as theologians tell us that each person has a "God-shaped vacuum" in her soul that only God can fill, daughters have a mom-shaped space in their head that will be taken up with thoughts of Mom. It doesn't really matter what the thoughts are, the space reserved for Momville will still be the same. If you had a great relationship with your mom, pleasant thoughts and great memories will be in your mom acreage. If you have experienced a strained relationship with her, then the acreage will have a few more rocks and weeds. If you have not known your mother at all, thoughts of her and her absence will fill that spot—what she must have been like and the constant disappointment that she could not be there for you.

A friend of mine who is adopted tells me that she spent a good deal of her childhood occupied—even obsessed—with thoughts of her birth mother. She wondered how her birth mom could have given her away and if she would ever reenter her life. My friend would play with her dollies and wonder why her mom chose to keep her other brothers and sisters but decided to release her for adoption. It wasn't until she was in her forties that she finally realized that the "mom space" in her head was so filled with thoughts of her birth mother that she never fully appreciated her adoptive mom until after she left home.

Country music singer Faith Hill has said that her need to meet her birth mother was a deep yearning in her during her young adult years and necessary for her to feel that she understood herself. Both of these women made clear that it was not due to any mistreatment or neglect by their adoptive moms, but just a deep (and natural) questioning about themselves, their history, their genetics, their origins.

My niece can relate somewhat to this. Her mother has been out of the picture since she was about two years old. Her mom would drift through about once a year to see my niece and somewhat pick the "scab" off the emotional wound. I think it must be terrible to be a child and to mentally stroll past a scorched piece of prime real estate reserved for Thoughts of Mom every day of your life. So Kristin has done something very difficult to do—she has trained herself not to think of her mother. But even the exhausting discipline of not thinking about her still takes brain space.

Some daughters won't ever know their birth mothers. Some mothers may not ever know their daughters. And for a good many of them, it will not be because of adoption or distance, it will be because they don't want to know each other—so they decide that the current stalemate of tolerance is preferable to true knowing. Like being lonely in a crowded room, you can feel motherless or daughterless while standing mere inches from each other. Some mothers and daughters are locked in such personal struggles between them that they wish they did not know each other.

Regardless of whether you know each other or not, choose to engage with each other or not, care for each other or not, the mother/daughter connection is a chunk of mental real estate that you will continue to land upon as you go around the game of life. Even an article in the *New York Times* reported, "New research has found that a mother's love is like a drug, 'a potent substance that cements the parent-infant bond and has a profound impact on later development.'"[1]

This brings us to an interesting and age-old conundrum of the mother/daughter relationship: We know that moms have an enormous influence in our lives, but part of us pushes back from

[1] From "Addicted to Mother's Love: It's the Biology, Stupid," *New York Times*, June 29, 2004.

it in our need for independence. We desperately want our adult autonomy but still crave the nurture that only a good mother can provide.

I believe one step we can all make toward healthy mother/daughter connections is to acknowledge the amount of prime real estate that our moms have in our heads and, if we are moms, be careful not to continue to expand that acreage unnecessarily. As a mom, I only want the acreage in my daughter's head that is accrued through heart-to-heart talks, shared experiences, family history, and frequent expressions of my love to her. I don't want to take up space in her head due to my insecurities, need to feel needed, and frequent guilt trips. I want her to *want* to visit my mental acreage often and to find a constantly appreciating piece of real estate every time she lands there.

the mother
✳ of
invention

Moms believe we can solve anything. Just ask any of us, we'll tell you straight up. It doesn't matter if it's an area we have any expertise in or not, or if we've ever encountered anything like it before. No matter. I Am Mother. If I don't know anything about it, I will just have to make something up. When the Mother in us rises up it trumps any doubts we would entertain. We may have self-confidence issues in other areas but don't even think about questioning our ability to come through in our child's hour of need.

I don't think this is something that is added to our personalities through hormones or the gestational process. If that were the case, adoptive mothers and Other Mothers would be deficient in this trait. No—this comes from abundant opportunity to prove ourselves worthy by children who are so distracted by the wonders of the world that they forget to mention that they need a science project started, charted, completed, and presented by second period tomorrow morning. Or maybe it's a fifth grader who sheepishly pulls a wadded up note out of her backpack dated *six weeks ago,* informing you that the school musical is tonight and your child (in the lead role, no less) will need a period-accurate costume. Whatever gray matter is left in a mom's brain instantly begins to regenerate worn-out synapses and someway, somehow, there is a colonial Patrick Henry costume, complete with cotton-ball-on-hairnet cornstarched wig stage-ready by 6 p.m.

Few children dare to approach their father in such a situation. They can predict that this would result in a lengthy lecture from The Man, which would include little sympathy or tolerance for excuses and would end with something akin to, "You've made your bed, now you'll have to lie in it." Kids know that moms manufacture more empathy than a snow machine makes fake flakes in Turin, Italy. We will marshal our resources, muster something up, and rise to the occasion.

The phrase "Necessity is the mother of invention" correctly identifies the mom as the one who can "git 'er done." Moms actually enjoy a good improvisation in a pinch. If we don't have the right tool we find a workable substitute in the junk drawer. If dads don't have the right tool they spend an afternoon at Home Depot.

There are even studies that show that lab rats that have given birth have a fundamental positive shift in the chemistry of their brains. This study seems to suggest that some interesting changes occur in the areas of female's cognitive and problem-solving skills as a result of having offspring. At the University of Richmond neuroscientist Craig Kinsley has published his studies showing that mother rats are smarter than the non-mother rats. They can find food faster and get through mazes more efficiently than rats without pups.

This is no surprise to me because moms, by job description, simply have to get more done in less time. We tend to be more creative thinkers and multitaskers at every level of creation.

Thus we now turn our attention to some creative, inventive women. We cannot say if they were inventors before they were mothers but (due to the rat study) we can say that motherhood must not have hindered their inventive prospects. We can also say a hearty "Thanks!" to these mothers of invention who solved a world of dilemmas for us all.

SARAH BREEDLOVE (MADAM C.J.) WALKER

She was born to recently freed slaves in 1867, orphaned at six and widowed at twenty, but Sarah Breedlove had no lack of ingenuity and ambition. She was an admirer of Booker T. Washington and knew that opportunity existed for someone with a good product who was willing to work hard. Sarah looked to her own heritage (her aunt was an herb doctor) to formulate something that would "improve the texture of African-American hair" and became the creator of an inventive method for straightening that employed a hot comb and emollient creams. (Note that this was during the same time that white girls were perming their hair within an inch of its life to get the wavy locks of the silent film stars — another proof that everybody wants somebody else's hair.) Sarah then trained her own sales force to sell door-to-door and an empire was born. Her line of hair products and her sales acumen have made Madam C. J. Walker's products a legendary staple for hairdressers and consumers alike, but perhaps her greatest contribution was her invention of such a large number of job opportunities for women of color at a time when hardly any existed.

ANN MOORE

When Ann was in the Peace Corps in West Africa she was able to observe how African mothers carried their babies slung around their bodies and how calm it made those children to feel so close to their mothers. (Of course, it could have been because they had them strapped to them so tightly that the babies couldn't cry, but let's not overanalyze.) As a young woman she wondered if mothers in the United States might benefit from this hands-free way to carry a child. When she became a mother herself she wanted to carry her baby the way the West Africans did, but found out that she must've been absent the day they taught the "how to tie your baby on" class as her baby kept slipping out (inventor babies usually get to be the test subjects—painful!). So she invited her mother to help her experiment with her designs to approximate what she saw in West Africa (which would give a whole new meaning to, "Look Ma, no hands!") that would keep the baby secure so that the mother could relax and go about her life. After several tries they came upon the design for the Snugli baby carrier, and for years now moms have been using it to free up their hands to chase after the older siblings.

MARY ANDERSON

This is one mother who took her glass cleaning and wiping skills to a whole new level. Southern belle Mary Anderson took a trip from her Birmingham, Alabama, home to The Big Apple in the winter of 1903 and took a big city ride on a fancy streetcar. She noticed that the streetcar operator had to get out and clean off the windshield at frequent intervals. Being a true southerner Mary thought it was awfully inconvenient to have to interrupt a lovely ride for scraping snow and ice off the windshield, and it was dangerous, too. (Moms are always concerned about anything that could be dangerous to any other mother's child.) She commenced to ponder the problem and hit upon an idea for a rubber blade placed on the outside of the vehicle (but operated from inside) that would swing across the window and sweep off any ice or snow that had accumulated. She had her idea patented in 1905 and windshield wipers were born. There's no way she could have known the impact she would have on the auto industry, not to mention the law enforcement community (where else would they stick parking tickets?).

BETTE NESMITH GRAHAM

This woman invented two very cool things. Her first invention would add value to the life of prepubescent girls from 1966-1969—her son, Michael Nesmith, large-sideburned member of the TV show band, The Monkees. You would think that this would have been enough to validate her existence on the planet, but this woman had at least one more thing to offer society. She also can lay claim to creating a second chance for electric typists everywhere. When Bette was an executive secretary she was happy to be typing on the newfangled electric typewriters, but found that the resulting pages could not be corrected because of the carbon ribbons. Like other typists she became frustrated over having to retype a whole page because of a single error. You know she wasn't the only one thinking, *"Good grief. I could have gone to the salon and had my hair done* three times *for all the hours I've wasted retyping these fool papers!"* So she put her Monkee-bearing brain upon it and created her product after observing painters who didn't remove mistakes but covered them with an additional layer of paint. After her home-based business got to be more than she could handle Bette patented Liquid Paper in 1958 and became a heroine to mistake-makers everywhere. Moral of her story: A mom would rather formulate, patent, manufacture, and market a new product than retype anything.

RUTH HANDLER

Here's a woman who had a thing for plastic. No, not the kind you charge with. She was into the Barbie kind. Actually, that was the nickname of her daughter, and her son's name was (what else?) Ken. Ruth, her husband, and a business partner started Mattel in their garage in 1946 making picture frames and doll furniture. Their company soon had some success with Burp Guns and Mouse Guitars (advertised on the Mickey Mouse Club TV shows). But Ruth was more interested in her daughter's preoccupation with paper dolls and she wondered why there were no three-dimensional dolls that would allow girls her daughter's age to act out their aspirations for the future. Being Californians they made her bust-to-waist-to-hip ratio with anatomically impossible standards, but the Barbie Doll overcame such issues to become one of the biggest success stories in toy manufacturing history. No matter your opinion of whether Barbie was a boon to girls' imaginations or the beginning of unattainable standards of beauty in our country, Ruth Handler also used her knowledge of plastics to help women who had undergone mastectomies. After her own battle with breast cancer in 1970, Ruth was disappointed in the prosthesis options that were available. She went to work to develop a breast prosthesis that was remarkably similar to the original and received a patent for her creation, "Nearly Me," in 1975.

FRANCES GABE

I have invented this in my head a million times, but Frances Gabe actually did it. This mother must have gotten good and fed up one day because she thought up the ultimate mother fantasy—a self-cleaning house. It seems that dear Frances was given to a strong engineering bent because this woman went to work creating a ten-inch-square "cleaning/drying/heating/cooling" unit in the ceiling of each room of her house. And this is no pie-in-the-Epcot-sky idea, because Frances Gabe has been living in her self-cleaning house for over forty years. Now, I have to say that I am a little confused as it seems that everything in it would have to be waterproof because, at the push of a button, the house turns into something akin to a car wash. Jets of soapy water wash the entire room, then rinse it, and the blowers dry any water that hasn't run down the center of the room drains. (I am wondering if you could stand your children in the middle of the room and let them get clean along with the room.) Where did this woman keep all her important papers and file her receipts? Can you imagine the conversation with the IRS agent? "No, really, sir. All my receipts were legible before I pushed the quick rinse cycle for the house. Just be glad I didn't choose the Hot Wax option." Each clothes closet is a washer-dryer combination (don't bother buying any dry cleanables), and when you put the dirty dishes in the kitchen cabinet, no worries because the cabinet is a dishwasher (obviously Frances had to do one too many sinkfuls of dishes as a child). I have to say that when we were looking for our home we didn't have any real estate agents show us any with the "total self-cleaning option" so I would imagine it would be many years before we could get this sort of George Jetson automation on our cul-de-sac.

But in the meantime, let's hear it for this woman who had a disdain for cleaning and the technical expertise to dispense with it!

JULIE NEWMAR

Of course when you see her name you immediately think "Catwoman" from the Batman show, but this TV star from the sixties and seventies was thinking of retaining her kittenish figure past its prime. This mom knew that if she needed a little assistance "bringing up the rear" then a lot of other women must be needing the same thing. Refusing to believe that the effects of gravity were without remedy, she introduced her patented improvement to pantyhose, "Nudemar", which consisted of ultra-tight construct with extra elastic in the fanny for additional control to the unplanned jiggle of the backside. Mothers everywhere rejoiced—that is, until they tried to pull them on.

MARION DONOVAN

If you reverse the order of the letters in the word "diaper" you get the word "repaid" — which is how women felt before Marion Donovan decided to turn her laundry frustration into a product that would change motherhood forever. She had an idea to make a plastic diaper cover that would keep her baby's bedding dry *and* protect her sanity from hanging those same sheets out on the clothesline day after day. From a plastic shower curtain she created a diaper cover that was waterproof. Her version of these rubber baby pants were superior to other previous designs because she used snaps (instead of safety pins). When she could drum up no interest from (male) manufacturers, Marion did what persistent mothers do: she refused to take no for an answer. Her patented "Boater" rolled out at Saks Fifth Avenue in 1949 and was an instant hit with moms.

Ultimately she decided to turn her creative attention to an even better solution — a real disposable diaper. You've got to hand it to a woman who is willing to put her first invention out of business for a better idea. She used her mom-knowledge of the problem and knew that she had to find a special kind of paper that would absorb water and not fall apart in the process. Marion spent a couple of years perfecting the initial prototype and took it to a variety of manufacturers in 1951 where it was met with the same rejection she had experienced with her Boaters. As she could find no takers she turned her attention to other inventions. It took ten years for the males in charge to catch up to her vision, and in 1961 a gentleman named Victor Mills used her prototype to develop the item that causes even non-Catholic mothers to genuflect—Pampers. Marion was a prolific inventor with patents for soap dishes that drain (well, duh!), a dental floss loop (who hasn't cut off their circulation trying to defeat plaque?), and a hanger that hangs up to thirty garments in the space of just one. Let us pause for a moment and give thanks for the foresight and determination of this Connecticut mom.

As long as the world keeps spinning, moms will keep trying to improve upon it. All these mothers model for us that when we are engaged in solving any problem we just might be making the world a better place for years to come.

✳ mom's top 10

S o it's a *slight* exaggeration, but over a lifetime as a mom you will give close to one million directions, add to that another one million reasons why your child needs to follow your directions, and *add to that* another million stories about how others did not follow their mother's directions and had to suffer the consequences for the rest of their ever-born days.

Kids wonder why their mothers are so repetitious and BOring, but the moms feel the need to repeat themselves because the kids aren't listening to them and kids don't listen to moms because they think moms are so repetitious. Do you see how we contribute to each other's insanity? And it does not matter how many times you have repeated yourself, because when it is time for your child to make her way into the world you will *still* stand there waving good-bye, wondering if you told them anything of importance, anything that really mattered, or anything they actually *needed* to know. This wondering will cause you to lose a couple of months' sleep. And if you ever do actually fall asleep you will wake with a start at 2 a.m. thinking something like, "*I wonder if I told her to always get a second estimate on any major car repair . . .*"

Sleep researchers tell us that women have from 20-50 percent higher incidence of insomnia than men. These sleep experts report that this is due to our fluctuating levels of estrogen. Women would tell you that this is REALLY because we are the only gender that truly has a grip on the emotional complexities of life and once the lights go out our minds zoom in like a laser pen on the most pressing issue de jour. Men always have the same solution to this problem as they yawn and say, "There's nothing you can do about it tonight, honey. Go to sleep." Oh, but that is where they are wrong, wrong, WRONG. We women can lie there and do LOTS of stuff about it in our heads. We have mock conversations where we think up all the wise counsel we are going to give should this pretend conversation ever materialize, we think up really great responses we SHOULD have said in prior conversations (where is that scriptwriter when you really need her?), we plan out scenarios and extrapolate potential endpoints and then we scrap certain ones and file others in the Possible Acceptable Outcomes. Guys just THINK there is nothing you can do about it at night, but that's just because they lack imagination. Plus they always start snoring right after their "nothing you can do about it tonight" pronouncement. With all that noise coming from the other side of the bed we couldn't get to sleep even if our brain could stop problem-solving in the dark.

I made up the list I'm about to give to you during one of those sleepless nights. It's a countdown a la *The David Letterman Show* of some things I probably should have told my kids before they got so big and know-it-all-already, and I might have told them these things in different ways over several years, but I just never sat down and codified the entries. It also came in handy when I was asked to speak at a baccalaureate service last spring. (I made the pre-grads yell out the countdown as we went along. I don't know if they absorbed any of the truth but they knew exactly how many points were left on the outline and none of them went to sleep, which constituted my measure of success regarding baccalaureates.) This list also works great as a laminated card to give kids before they fly the coop, but if you sit down and try to *tell* them these things any time before they have children of their own you may get several eyerolls before you finish.

MOM'S TOP 10 LIST

10. Surround yourself with people who build you up.

This is a difficult concept for young adults. They tend to be idealistic and want to believe that everyone has pure motives and a good heart and the best intentions. They think everyone is interested in helping each other because the people in their group of friends have never all been up for the same promotion. It takes a couple of toxic friend experiences to let you know that there are more than a few negative people in this world, and they are not the ones who will keep your thoughts elevated and moving in the right direction. This is not to say that we surround ourselves with people who are not authorized and deputized to call us on the carpet when we mess up, just that they are doing it because they truly love and respect us — not to tear us down and humiliate us. And sometimes WE are our own worst enemy and very hard on ourselves. If we have encouraging people in our lives we can balance our inner critic with someone who believes in us.

9. Take care of your body.

Another hard concept for young adults who see themselves as immortal. It's not just that they take unnecessary risks, kids don't understand that the body is a sensitive machine that needs TLC to run optimally. The need to rest, eat right, exercise, floss, lay off the sugar and caffeine, and so on, is totally unappreciated by the young. They believe that their body will take whatever they throw at it (a steady diet of Pop-Tarts, Diet Coke, and Ramen Noodles) and just keep on ticking like a Timex watch. Which explains why there is such a prevalence of mononucleosis in first-semester freshmen girls. It's not all the kissing—it's the no-sleep, junk food, stressed-out life-style. Suddenly your body rebels and says in no uncertain terms, "If you're not going to give me the rest I need, I'll just bench you for a while 'til I get it." My kids make fun of me because I have a theory that increasing your water consumption and sleep will cure anything. Got a cold? More water, more sleep. Got the flu? More water, more sleep. Got zits? More water, more sleep. Of course if you drink much more water than usual you will have to get up a lot during the night to let it out. This might defeat the directive of "more sleep," but logic has never been an issue for me. (Just ask my kids.) I do believe that God gave our bodies the ability to repair themselves if we give them a chance. My kids say that I think the more water/more sleep prescription is the cure for everything—even cancer (who knows?).

I just don't want my kids to have neglected their bodies to the point that, when they finally get clear about their purpose on earth, they no longer have the energy or health to accomplish it. Your body is the way you get around in this world—so (physically) it is your only vehicle. Do not leave your vehicle unattended. All unattended vehicles will be ticketed and towed. Your body is the temple of God who lives inside you. Do not let that temple fall into ruins.

8. You make your decisions—but then your decisions make you.

One of the cool things you can learn in biology class (other than the fact that fruit flies have frighteningly short life spans—one to two weeks! Imagine all the things they have to cram in) is that the top layer of your skin is replaced every twenty-one days. Every three weeks—all new epidermis. Which is not quite as exciting when you stop to think that we are constantly shedding skin cells everywhere, all day. This makes us all "flakey" (literally). Interestingly enough twenty-one days is the exact time psychologists tell us it takes to break old habits and establish new ones. It's like your top layer can be changed both ways—how you look and how you act. One thing that defines the term "young" is the inability to see how, really, there are no insignificant decisions. They all add up to the sum of what eventually becomes Your Life. Perhaps that's why we have midlife crises—we wake up one day and realize that we have made a series of decisions that have led us someplace we never intended to end up. The great thing is this (because we always have the power to choose and choose again): It's never too late to do the right thing. In the movie *Where the Heart Is,* Novalee tells her friend, who is asking how to explain a difficult situation to her children, "You tell them that our lives can change with every breath we take." Thank God for that.

7. A chapter of Proverbs a day keeps the stupids away.

I have no idea if the writer of Proverbs or the organizers of the Bible had any idea that they were helping us get some daily wisdom in an easy-to-keep-track-of format, but you never have to wonder which proverbs you are supposed to be reading on which day. There is one chapter of Proverbs for every day of the month. If you divide up the word it's "pro" (positive) + "verbs" (action words). These are not just principles we absorb—they are actions we take to keep from living a stupid life. "Proverbs" become that way because they are time-tested principles that keep us from making the same old mistakes that everyone before us has made. It's like a relief map of the common roads of life, complete with orange safety cones surrounding the potholes with sirens blaring and neon signs flashing, "Danger! Don't step here!" The least we could do is make some fresh mistakes—but according to Proverbs there are precious few of those.

6. Keep your destiny in mind.

Life has a way of interrupting our plans. We get derailed, off track, undone. Happily, none of this is connected to our destiny. Destiny is closely tied to the concept of "purpose," but destiny specifically connotes that God has another set of plans that super-sede our own and draw us into His-story. Webster defines *destiny* as "a predetermined course of events often held to be an irresistible power or agency." Keeping your destiny in mind means that everything you choose to engage your life in (time, energy, resources) must be worth it and that decisions should be made with the awareness that Something Else is usually going on above and beyond the results you can see immediately. Sometimes our greatest destiny is in the little things done well and with great love. That's another interesting thing about the concept of destiny—you never know if The Small Thing is really The Big Thing cleverly disguised.

5. Pray about everything.

Paul thought this concept was important enough that it bore repeating in his letters to the fledgling churches. "Don't worry about anything. Pray about everything" (Philippians 4:6 TLB). Does this mean that The God of the Universe is interested in the minutiae of my life? Absolutely. If it's on your mind He wants to hear about it. This is the intimate Abba (Daddy) connection. In fact, a great way to think about it is if you were to sit down with your dad, maybe not the one you were born with (especially if you aren't close to him), but your ideal dad—the one you wish you had—and he said to you, "Girl—tell me what's been happening with you lately. What's on your mind?" And then you start telling him what all has happened to you and how you feel about it and your concerns about all kinds of things, from the tiny matters to the ones that seem overwhelming. This is how we can learn to "worry our prayers"—or "pray our worries"—meaning the moment that a thought starts circling around in our brain and crosses the boundary from "wonder" to "worry" that is the time to shove it over another category to "prayer." That is precisely what Paul is saying—move from worry to prayer. After a while this will become habit (twenty-one days!) and we see that the worry is useless but the prayer is powerful. In the movie *Shadowlands* there is a conversation between C.S. Lewis and his friend Harry:

> **Harry:** "Christopher can scoff, Jack, but I know how hard you've been praying; and now God is answering your prayers."
> **Lewis:** "That's not why I pray, Harry. I pray because I can't help myself. I pray because I'm helpless. I pray because the need flows out of me all the time, waking and sleeping. It doesn't change God, it changes me."

4. Never make important decisions when you are tired or hungry.

Everything looks worse when you're tired or hungry. Most diet experts will tell you that you shouldn't even go to the grocery store if you are tired and hungry because you will end up with a cart full of stuff that you think will make you feel better but isn't nutritious. If you aren't qualified to make grocery decisions in a hungry/sleepy mental state, then that should give you a clue as to the foolishness of making any other decisions when you are sleep- or food-deprived. If you are tired and hungry you are really someone else. You are the weakest version of yourself, and that is no time to be making any sort of decision, much less an important one. You will be driven by short-term thinking instead of long-term planning. Then you will make bad decisions and we know what that leads to (see number 8).

3. Take the time to decide what is worth doing, then do it with your whole heart and with excellence. Avoid shortcuts as they are usually full of potholes.

And the challenge lies in the first three words: "take the time." Part of the folly of youth is to feel that you have all the time in the world, yet not to spend any of it on considering your priorities and then taking the time to do what is important with commitment and excellence. These are the things that separate people who are living their life with a sense of destiny from those who are not. People without destiny are usually half-hearted and mediocre. They want the shortest route to completion and don't really care if they ever get there. They look for shortcuts and usually find them, but not without stumbling along the way.

2. Call home.

It's good for extraterrestrials and for offspring: "ET phone home." What kids don't realize is that parents don't really give a rip if our children have anything important to say. We just want to hear your voice and know that you are okay. If you have any actual information to impart that is considered Total Gravy. I tell my kids to keep a notepad somewhere where they can see it every day and jot down something that happened that day that only a mom would care about. At the end of two or three days there should be at least a couple of entries and, voila, conversational fodder! However, you *can* just call and say, "Hi, Mom. I love you," and then just breathe on the other end of the phone line and we would think it was a great conversation. Just call to let us know that you still know the number. I don't have to call my mother (unless you count yelling down the hall to tell her something as "calling"), but this principle is true for kids of all ages. Just ask any of your friends whose mom is no longer on this earth. They'll tell you exactly what they would give to be able to pick up the phone and talk with Mom about anything/nothing/everything one more time.

1. Love God.

There is nothing that makes a mom happier than to see that her kids have a firm grasp on what it means to love God. That would mean that you know Him, love to be in His Word, love to get together with other believers to worship Him and study the Bible together, and that you are loving people that aren't particularly loveable. And that you are tuned in to His voice that can lead you through the rest of your life instead of just the voice of your parents, who, despite their love for you, won't always be there.

I am happy to report that my college boys are swimming along nicely in most of the areas on my Top 10 List. Austin doesn't get enough sleep and Calvin is always hungry, which, according to my list, means that neither should EVER make any decisions. And my caller-ID doesn't register their names every day, but they call occasionally (sniff, sniff). I am hopeful for my girlie-girl, Elyse, as she already eats a somewhat balanced diet and takes time to make important decisions. When she does sally forth on her own, I hope she will carry with her a strong sense of identity, a heart full of love—and, most important to her mama, her cell phone with my number set to autodial.

returning ✳ to the mother ship

Novelist Thomas Wolfe told us that "you can't go home again." This is true if the place you grew up has been bulldozed over and they have built a Wal-Mart over the top of your old neighborhood. But if your old homeplace is still there, then (technically) you *can* go home again. It just won't ever be the same as you remember it. It's like your former world gets dipped in Shrinky Dink coating, popped into the oven, and comes out looking smaller than you recall. The staircase doesn't look so tall, the trees aren't as high, the yard looks smaller. The people who inhabited your world grew up and got real jobs. Things changed and life went on. This is most evident when you have been gone quite a while.

I have not been able to go back to any of my early childhood homes. The one in which I grew up burned to the ground from an electrical fire the year after my mom remarried. My grandpa had passed away a couple of years before and my Nana was then obliged to move into town. There weren't that many photos of me as a child to begin with but most that did exist were lost to the fire.

There are a few school pictures (is it that school photographers take the shot for the maximum goofy look quotient? Or are we all just that goofy looking our whole school life? And do school photographers later end up working at DMVs?), but no photos of me *doing* anything. This is probably due to the fact that when I was growing up kids didn't really have to do anything. They were just kids. You know—they *played*. And no adults took pictures of *that* because film was expensive back then. If someone was going to snap a picture you had to be doing something really important, like receiving a medal from the president of the United States. We did not have team pictures from T-ball, pictures from ballet recital, or photos from spring break in Cancun. This is because where and when I grew up there was no such thing as T-ball or ballet lessons, and spring break simply meant no school so that we could play all day. My boy cousins would come out to the farm and spend the whole day trying to pick cockleburs off the mama cow's coat and then shimmying up trees to escape their wrath. We would throw chinaberries down from the trees and bother Nana for something to eat every twenty minutes. Not really photo material.

There's a part of me that is very grateful for that kind of long, slow, unstructured childhood. Nowadays it is almost nonexistent as everybody runs kids from activity to activity to lesson to practice to activity with no time to get bored. I firmly believe that it's a *good* thing for kids to get bored. It's a marker for them on the Boredom to Exhilaration Continuum. If you are stimulated and overscheduled all the time, how can you know what real excitement feels like? And if you're never bored as a kid, what do you have to look forward to in adult life? That used to be one of the main inducements to grow up, so that you could schedule exciting things for yourself and no one was going to be able to stop you.

As a parent I intentionally taught my kids this value. They could choose one activity per quarter and that was it. And woe unto the child that came to me and said, "Mom, I'm bored." I wanted my kids to learn that I was not the Funtime Activity Director of the Renfroe Cruise Line, so I had a list of "Bored Chores" that were available anytime anyone could not think up a way to entertain themselves. I only had to use it once per child.

Among the few photos from my childhood there were no photos of family vacations, either. That's because when I was growing up we didn't have vacations. That's right. Vacations were for rich people. And we were not rich people. We went for "visits" instead of vacations. The difference between them is that on a "vacation" you go to a destination and enjoy the local attractions and environs. On a "visit" you only go to towns where relatives live because you stay with them and enjoy their house. We always went to see my Aunt Wanda because she lived in Dallas in a ritzy neighborhood and she had a pool. I cannot overemphasize how impressive that was to me as a child. Our whole hometown only had one community pool, so for people who were somehow related to me to have their own pool, well, that was just too cool for school.

The first time I can remember going to see my aunt and uncle I was about five years old. I had never been around a pool before and I thought I could swim just because I had seen people do it on TV (I mean, how hard could it be?). So I jumped in and proceeded to flail and inhale a gallon of chlorinated water. My Uncle J.B. fished me out before I expired and explained to me the benefits of the shallow end. Although I have no photo of that moment I can still feel the hot humiliation on my face as I realized that some things really are much harder than they look on TV.

When my mom remarried we moved out to a fish hatchery for a couple of years and then to Ft. Worth to live on another fish hatchery next to Carswell Air Force Base. Those were both small government-issue houses. I've never been back to either of them. We then moved to a starter home in Burleson, Texas, fully equipped with green shag carpet, avocado appliances, and a big crepe myrtle tree in the front yard. As it is with government workers, if you want to move up the GS ladder you must be willing to relocate, so we made a big move to Virginia. Our home there was much bigger than our last (2,000 square feet!) and it had a picture window that looked out on our yard—which seemed to be the length of a football field by the time it reached the street. Mind you, I was in high school at the time so my perception should not have been so off, but about ten years later when I drove past that house I was convinced that they had moved the road. It was just a few yards from the house to the street! What happened to the rest of the field? Seems that bushes and grass and landscaping happened to it. And time.

You can go back home again, but it's all different. Nothing can really prepare you for the Twilight Zone feeling you get as you park your car in the driveway and make your way toward the front door. As you exit your vehicle you start out feeling like the age that is printed on your driver's license. You may be a very independent individual who has made your way in the world and is doing quite nicely for yourself, thank you very much. You may have a nice financial portfolio, a great place of your own where you reside, and friends who love and respect you. But with every step you take between your car and the front door you start to feel less independent, less grown up. You might as well subtract three years off the age you are for every step you take until you reach for the front door handle. When you open that door to your former digs you have usually regressed to somewhere around fourteen years old.

I call this the Chronological Shrinking Syndrome. What is its underlying cause? You are about to be back on HER TURF. This is Mama's House and you are now all but powerless because she has The Home Court Advantage.

Now I'm sure that Mama doesn't mean to Shrinky Dink you. It just happens. This is the place where she has scolded and molded you. It's where you got lectured on a regular basis. It's the place you made some dumb pronouncements and the same place you tried to escape your childhood. You start falling into your old patterns of thinking and feeling quite apart from your will. You wonder how you could possibly feel this immature again. You are stricken with the distinct feeling that whatever amount of time you agreed to stay is probably too long.

Let me hasten to say that none of this is because you don't love your mom or want to spend time with her; it's just that when you step into your childhood home the Chronological Shrinking Syndrome sweeps over you and compromises all the ground you have gained as an adult. Every time you turn around there are pictures of you at stages you hoped no one would remember, much less frame. There are reminders in every nook and cranny of your awkward growing years — the acne, the bad hair, the braces. Of course your mom treasures your development at every age, but these Shrines to Adolescent Angst compound your regression. And should you bring home a friend or fiancé you will see your mother act out your episode on "Mom's Biography Channel" right there in your old living room. At this point you may be feeling like it should be called The Dying Room.

For mothers the shrines start, innocently enough, with the refrigerator. This appliance is in every American home and its obvious use is to keep the milk cold and other food items from spoiling. Before women become mothers the fronts of refrigerators are used for only two things: a memo to their husband and the grocery list. It's simple, uncluttered, and functional. Then one day the same woman comes home with a baby and *BAM!* the refrigerator becomes Grand Central Station and the two magnets that worked so well are now totally inadequate to keep up with demand. There are memos on pediatrician appointments, immunization dates, types of formulas and diapers, coupons for Wet Wipes and apple juice and, stuck somewhere in the midst of these important notes is the seed of what will become a bumper crop — baby's hospital picture. It's just one at first. One tiny photo of the newest member of the household. It seems so innocent. Yet contained in that one little photo is tremendous power — the power to overtake the entire surface of this refrigerator with kindergarten artwork, photos from T-ball teams, appointment cards, handmade holiday cards, report cards, and all manner of miscellany that eventually gets put into your Personal Effects Chest. This is because moms have no way to decide which things are worth saving and which things need to be tossed. Mom's motto: "If my baby touched it, it should be archived."

For some women this sentiment turns into an all-out addiction to scrapbooking. These are the mothers who are *really prepared* for the session of sharing your history with a potential future family member. And your boyfriend or fiancé will assure you that they think it's charming to stroll with your mother down memory lane, but your innards are having a cringe-fest. You smile weakly as she is killing you softly. And should you protest in any way you will get the Martyred Mother Look, which then obligates you to a much higher ticket Mother's Day gift.

Then there is the issue of your old room. Has your mom chosen to freeze it in time? Has she kept everything exactly as you left it? Like a little museum to you? There are a couple of schools of thought on this subject. Some moms like to keep everything as it was to make you feel like your room is always there. Should you send an eventual grandchild to sleep over, they can soak up some ambience from your childhood. But should *you* have to sleep in a frozen-in-time room you can be sure that you will only regress further emotionally.

Then there are the moms who actually start a mental timer the moment you reach eighteen and count the days 'til the statute of limitations runs out on you occupying your space. Mom is just itching to get rid of your stuff—remember, all those treasures she dragged out to the garage for the annual family yard sale and you sneaked back in? Now it's about to be history, kiddo. You are soon to be outta sight and that means your stuff is up for disposal. Mom's got PLANS for that room, baby! There will be a massive cleaning out, redecorating, and reclaiming of space. For these moms "empty nest" is not such a trauma—it's an opportunity for a workout room!

There will always be reasons to go home again—family reunions, holidays, weddings, funerals, births, birthdays, celebrations—the things that tie families together. Just prepare yourself to be knocked slightly off center as you return to the mother ship.

Live long and prosper.

so which
*one of us
is crazy?

If you want to skip this chapter I can summarize it for you:

Both of you are.

All of us are.

Mothers and daughters are crazy. Flat out crazy. We are crazy because we came that way, and we are crazy because we make each other that way. That's why it's possible to feel a million different ways about each other all the time. We are complicated, sometimes strange people. We are *women*, after all.

My mother can drive me nuts. For example . . .

- She doesn't ever let the laundry finish drying—she always hangs it out on the deck for the last 20 percent (when the weather is good), so it looks like the Clampetts just moved in.
- She washes her hair and brushes her teeth in the kitchen sink but won't put dirty dishes in there. Instead, she stacks them up on the counter ledges so the sink will be "clean."

(And I paid good money for extra deep sinks so that the dishes could be off the countertops and out of sight . . . *in the sink* while awaiting Elyse's unloading of the dishwasher so we can reload it!)

- She will be up two hours before me and never touch the morning paper, but as soon as I sit down to read it she will come over and start taking pieces of the paper out from under me so that I have to keep track of which ones I've read and which ones I haven't. Then she'll sit there and wait for me to finish the next section (like I'm not reading fast enough).

On the other side of the Momwich, I drive my daughter crazy.

- I'm late for everything (which totally frazzles Elyse's "punctual" nature).
- I'm a professional lecturer.
- I'm terrible with directions. (I can be in the same hotel for five days and never really know where my room is.)
- I take books to read at sporting events.
- And, of course, I always think I'm right.

The good news is that all of our mother/daughter craziness is not necessarily bad news. If our relationships were neat and tidy and easy and fine we might be able to discount and dismiss each other. As it is we are locked in a continual process of building, admiring, analyzing, demolishing, repairing, and restructuring this primal relationship all the time. By the time we get to a nice level spot where we can really enjoy it for a while, something happens that shakes the thing up and we start all over again. We are constantly challenged to come into a loving, grace-filled dance with a mom who has known us since before we knew ourselves or a daughter who has stretched us in ways we never knew we could stretch. Every mom has a mental list of the things she hopes for her daughter. Every daughter has a list of how she wishes she could interact with her mom. Mostly no one gets everything on her list. The truth is, none of us is such a bargain. We are all flawed and emotionally handicapped. Some of us just don't know it or don't want to face it.

I feel positive that some of you may have hoped that contained in this book would be The List of a bunch of ways to improve your relationship with your mother or with your daughter. I wish I knew anyone who had that definitive list. I've heard some pretty great suggestions that include giving up unrealistic expectations, giving each other plenty of love and space, and refraining from using the word "should" in any conversation. But as good as those are, I don't know that they address the whole scope of the mother/daughter dance. I do know that the Bible has life-giving principles on every page, many of them that apply to *all* relationships, but none that specifically say, "Hey mothers, don't drive your daughters insane," or "Hey daughters, lighten up with your mom — she's human, you know." But there are principles of sacrificial love, mutual honor, preferring another over yourself, quick forgiveness, and tenderness that are held up as Standard Operating Procedures for all who follow Christ.

The question remains, if we are engaged in this lifelong mother/daughter dance, how then shall we dance? Will it be stilted and strained like a sixth grade slow dance? — touching each other just enough to acknowledge that we are partners without actually embracing? Or will we dance on opposite sides of the floor, hearing the same music but choosing to respond alone? Or will we look at our emotional feet, counting steps and concentrating on the form at the expense of the fun? Is it okay to say to the other, "You're squeezing me too tight," or will that make the other walk away? Perhaps we'll get locked in a single pattern and never be able to abandon it for moments of valuable improvisation.

Or maybe, just maybe, we could listen to the music together and teach each other new moves as the soundtrack of our lives changes from day to day and year to year.

One difficulty daughters struggle with is our inability to look beyond seeing Mom in a role to seeing her as another woman — a woman we might have chosen to be friends with had we not been family. Perhaps a good question to ask ourselves as daughters is, How would we view our mom if she were someone else's mom? Would we think she was weird? Or would we term her "enchanting" or "eclectic"? Every daughter is slightly embarrassed by her mother. I don't care if you have the coolest, hippest mom in the world. Even *that* will embarrass you — her attempts to *stay* cool and hip. My daughter loves me yet still gets all flustered when I slaughter slang in front of her friends. My mom loved her mom immensely, but my Nana's penchant for chatting up any and everyone she came in contact with embarrassed my mom.

A question for pondering: Would all the things that drive us up the wall about each other just become interesting personality characteristics if those characteristics had not been fully operational in our everyday life? When other people describe my mom to me I listen and think, "I vaguely recognize the woman they're talking about . . . yes, that's my mom." And it causes me to wonder why I can't seem to disassociate myself far enough from her to see her the same way her friends do. But it's because *she's my mom.* And perspective is difficult to come by when everything is so close.

To the daughters reading this I ask, How well do you know your mother as a person? What do you know of her life before you were born? Her hopes and aspirations? How she met your father? What she loves? Hates? Her dreams that got derailed in the process of living? What she remembers about her childhood? Her current dreams for the rest of her life? What she wants to accomplish in the time she has left on earth? Could you try to find a place in your heart that wants to know her *as another woman* instead of assuming that you know everything about her just because you lived a portion of your lives together?

I can tell you that the first time I realized that my mom was a woman (rather than defining her through her role in my life) was in the days and weeks after my dad died. She was immensely broken and undone because they were *so joined.* The difference in her was not just because of her grief and sorrow for her loss of Dad, but I literally saw her become a different person because she could no longer see herself reflected in his eyes of love. She lost a part of herself, an important definition of herself, because he was gone.

When it became clear to me that she was grieving over losing him for more reasons than I had imagined, I finally really *saw* her and realized that she was a woman who had lost the love of her life. I didn't see Mom. I saw Kay, another woman like me. Not a powerful symbol of nurturing and influence over me, but a woman with similar feelings and experiences who wanted nothing more than to see her reflection in Johnny's eyes one more time and now had to wrestle with the reality that it wasn't ever going to happen again.

That was the *first time* I saw her as a woman other than Mom. I was thirty-eight and she was fifty-eight.

Did my new insight change everything all at once? Not a chance. Did it cause a subtle shift in my perception that continues to shape our relationship even now? Definitely.

I'm sure there are many women reading this who have been hurt by their mother or by their daughter. Deeply. What do we do with the mound of hurts and disappointments that stand between us? Pretend it never got heaped up there in the first place? Act like it doesn't matter anymore? Ignore it? Find a way to navigate around it? Some of us choose to fixate on it—and look at the entire relationship through the frame of a single incident or time period. Any one incident or series of events is not our whole relationship, but, being human, we take our mental snapshots from the past and then enlarge them and frame them and hang them on the wall in our emotional foyer. Then every day when we go by, we look at them, touch them, and filter every word that is spoken in our current relationship through the freeze-frames of the past.

Others of us have a penchant for picking at emotional scabs.

Time and distance attempt to allow some measure of healing, but we can't stop ourselves from reopening the wounds. We want someone to acknowledge that we have been hurt, and we are not satisfied with a scar. We need the wound to stay open so our trauma will remain visible.

Truth is liberating. Jesus said, "I am the way and the truth and the life," (John 14:6, NIV) and "You will know the truth, and the truth will set you free" (John 8:32, NIV). You must be able to tell the truth about your life and be honest about the things that have happened. Having said that, I also think it's a big misconception that you can't have a *real* relationship if you don't go back and "fix" everything. No matter how many times you peel the onion (and let me say, I am all for peeling the onion—just know that it *will* make you cry) there will forever be things that are not resolvable. That's the legacy of The Fall.

Here is the *really* liberating truth: Everything is not going to get fixed and healed in this lifetime—that's what Heaven is for. You have to decide what can go under the mercy of God (not to be confused with "under the rug"—because when stuff is swept under the rug, it always sneaks back out and eventually makes a gargantuan mountain that you can't navigate around). Under the mercy of God is a place where you put things when you know that they are not going to be healed in this lifetime. These are the things you can't fix in your mom or in your daughter and they just need mercy. Grace. Forgiveness. And that is a perfectly okay place to start building something new—on the platform of mercy, forgiveness, and grace.

But you have to *decide* to put the new understructure there. In other words, you cannot deal with your mother issues until you deal with *The Father* issue. If you have never experienced God's unconditional love and radical forgiveness in your life, you will not be able to fully forgive anyone else. You cannot impart what you have not received. If you need to know God's amazing grace for yourself, then I encourage you to start with the Gospel of John in the Bible. It talks about true love and forgiveness and how God sacrificed His own son for our sin debt and wants us to experience radical forgiveness for ourselves and then give it away to others. Yes, even those closest to us who might have done us real harm. We all have "junk in the trunk"—the baggage and hurt that accompanies living. Your choice is whether you will put it up in the front seat, ask God to help you deal with it, allow Him to heal you from it, release it, and even laugh about it . . . or leave it in the trunk to rot and make you sick.

And what is your level of commitment to peeling the onion? Emotional excavation is difficult and grueling. Some of it is inevitable. It will happen as you face certain crises in your life. Do you want to "dredge" it all up? What is the potential improvement quotient? Only you know. I have a friend who went to counseling and therapy for years to deal with all the emotional hurt with her mother. Her mom refused to engage and let her clear up any of it directly. My friend maintains that it was helpful for her even though her mom never acknowledged any of it.

The question is: As mothers and daughters do you feel that it is essential to fix everything before you can have a healthy, growing relationship? Or is it possible for you to realize that we are a conglomeration of generations of broken people and that we can find the grace and courage within us to grapple with what we can *realistically* expect of each other? Let me ask it another way: If your mom or daughter were a quadriplegic would you expect her to take out the garbage or help you hang wallpaper? Of course not—you could see her handicap and determine that would not be something you could realistically expect from her. You would just say to yourself, "No matter how much I want her to help me with that she just isn't equipped for the task," and then you'd look to someone else to help you with that particular thing. The same holds true for us emotionally. Why do we keep looking to certain people to provide certain things for us when, in reality, they just don't have the capability? And let's face it: we are *all* emotionally challenged in some area. If we choose to see the people we love through eyes of understanding about how difficult certain things are for them, we will naturally have more compassion, patience, and forgiveness.

By the time we know enough to blame our moms for the problems they caused because of how they raised us, they are much more emotionally evolved women, so we tend to judge them based on "how could she do that to me when she obviously knows better?" Well, *now* they do, but back then they were probably doing the best they could for us with the information they possessed at the time. Plenty of mistakes get made on both sides of the mother/daughter relationship, but these do not have the power to define the future or our relationship unless we refuse the healing balm of forgiveness between us.

Another problem with the whole mother/daughter deal is that we really want a couple of easy suggestions that will heal years of difficulty and damage in a week or less. Apart from a miracle of God that's not possible. But each of us can pay attention to the other and make tiny, micromillimeter movements that can eventually lead to a major shift. If you take a gun (please don't—it's just an illustration) and you make an eighth of an inch adjustment in your aim it doesn't seem like such a big deal. But if you follow the course of that bullet over 100 yards it would be a pretty big correction. The same thing works in relationships—you don't have to make a huge move to get big results, just little movements over the course of time. If you start with small, manageable changes and stick with them you can make real progress toward the relationship you need. One day you both realize that things are going really well and neither of you can put her finger on exactly what's made it better. That's the kind of change that lasts, the kind that's real.

Does this mean that we are going to stop driving each other crazy? I don't think so. It may mean that we will be doing most of the same crazy stuff but we will be able to laugh with each other about it instead of fuming about it and highlighting our differences and weaknesses. There's a chance that if we could just relax and stop trying to fix each other all the time we might find a place of mutual delight *because* we know each other intimately, not in spite of it.

Okay, so if it's not one thing it's your mother. But it's real. It's drama. It's love. It's worth it.

a word
from
my mother

(Author's note: I did not pay my mother to write this, but I might add that she's in her sixties and will probably be needing me to choose her nursing home in the next decade or so. You may want to take that into account when reading the following.)

When Anita was born I would not let her feet touch the floor until she was a year old, and I would have preferred that she never did. This was partly out of fear that she would eat things off the floor but also because I was overly protective of her. Because I made such a bad choice in marrying her father and the marriage didn't work out, I spent a lot of my young mom years trying to make it up to my daughter. I didn't realize that wasn't really possible. In the process of us both growing up together Anita may have lost some of her childhood innocence and had to mature a little earlier than most kids. But she became a strong young girl.

When Anita was very young we all knew that she was gifted musically and we recognized that she was able to express herself creatively. I remember the first time I realized what a gift she had was when she was in the third grade musical *The Wizard of Oz* in the role of Dorothy and she was feeding all the other kids their lines. Anita has always had a strong sense of going for whatever she decided she needed to do whether she had any encouragement or not. She always did well in school without any help from me.

We remained close through her high school years because we spent time singing in a trio as a family. My greatest aspiration was to make a good home for her and Johnny. My mother always sacrificed for her children and I wanted to offer my life in the same way in service to Anita's family. I think it is important for any generation to see that there is someone who is willing to give of themselves, someone who believes in them — because that is ultimately what God does for us.

I so loved my mother for being that kind of person — the one who was cooking, sewing, loving, mending all her children. We have a world full of people who have no sense of anyone who feels that way about them. When you have that kind of example lived out before you like I had in my mom it inspires you to want to be that sort of person.

I have to say that, when you come to this point in your life, it's a little hard to change gears, but I am learning to do it a little at a time. It is such a joy to see Anita's ministry come into its own. I've always known that sharing her gifts with the world on a broad level was what she was destined to do, and it is hard to keep up with all that is going on. It's something new just about every day!

People say that when you find what you love to do you will

have a very fulfilled life. I've always loved cooking and laundry and helping people. Helping others is a joy to me in the same way that comedy is joy to Anita. When I went to work in retail it just validated that helping others really is my gift—both outside and inside the home.

When I get to watch Anita on stage I realize that her greatest gift is that she is an intimate communicator. The connection she has with people is very rare. I've always known it was there and wanted everyone else to experience it, too. I am proud of my daughter and only wish that I could share these moments with my mother. She was a big part of who I am, who Anita is, and who Elyse will become.

I believe in the amazing power of the mother/daughter connection and hope this book will help strengthen that bond for women of all generations.

Kay

acknowledgments

The author wishes to thank (and, this being a mother book, may also want to spank):

My mom (Kay) and daughter (Elyse) who have allowed me to publish our relationship foibles to the world. And we can all agree that there's a boatload of stuff that's way more interesting that only WE will ever know (at least until Elyse writes *her* book . . .).

My Only Ever Squeeze (John) who made me the mother I am and is reported to have enjoyed it.

My boys (Calvin and Austin) who had front-row seats to the Momwich and will be better men for having witnessed it all. Yes, women ARE mysterious. Three generations of women under the same roof? Positively alien. Having to deal with only one woman in your future marriage will seem like a skate. You can thank us later.

My Other Mothers (Vesta R., Faye B., Jean N., Maizie J.) who
  bring their own special brand of mothering to my life—I
  love you and thank God for you.

Nana—who had the love and strength to begin a new generation of God-lovers.

Traci Mullins—Editor without Equal. You are my nonnego-
  tiable. It's in writing. Next time we hold out for writing
  time in Jamaica. Or Italy. I'm not picky.

Terry Behimer, Dan Rich, and the whole NavPress crew—you
  champion the best in your authors. Thank you for believing in me.

Don Pape—Trusted advisor and Total Kwan Ambassador.

My church family at Destiny Metropolitan Worship Church
  and Pastor Bryan and Mrs. Lanette Crute. Serving the
  Lord with you guys is a joy.

And finally, to cover all my bases, I acknowledge everyone
  AND their mother.

about the
author

Anita Renfroe is a woman who has a gift for saying the things most every woman *thinks* but is afraid to *say*. She is a girl-friend's girlfriend and loves to get women together to celebrate All Things Female, All Things Funny. That is why people read her books, show up to her live performances, and buy her comedy concert DVDs. If laughter is good medicine, Anita's humor is like a protein shake for the soul. Her contagious joy should be monitored by the Centers for Disease Control, but it seems they aren't interested in things that are good for you.

Anita is ecstatically married to John and mom to several stellar young adults (Calvin, Austin, and Elyse). If you need to know more than that about her, visit her very rowdy website www.anitarenfroe.com.

ADD SOME PURSE-ONALITY TO YOUR LIFE.

Anita Renfroe pulls no punches as she gives women an ultimatum: hilarity or insanity? Take a look at the sorts of things that could drive a person crazy—if only they weren't so funny! These laugh-out-loud reflections remind women that God gives His children thousands of reasons to be joyful and full of hope.

Discover why re-gifting is trickier than it used to be, the Southern wisdom of leaving holiday lights up all year, and why holiday destinations that require mid-winter spray-on tans should be avoided. Full of humor, candor, and sass, Anita shows that chaotic holidays are a universal experience and encourages readers to step back and laugh at the craziness of the season.

Visit your local Christian bookstore, call NavPress at 1-800-366-7788, or log on to www.navpress.com to purchase.

To locate a Christian bookstore near you, call 1-800-991-7747.

NAVPRESS

BRINGING TRUTH TO LIFE

www.navpress.com

ANITA RENFROE LIVE FROM ATLANTA.

Purse-onality DVD

Anita Renfroe   1-60006-084-6

Available September 2006

Share the fun of seeing Anita Renfroe in concert with her new DVD, *Purse-onality*. In this hilarious experience, women of all ages will love keeping up with Renfroe as she proves it really is true that when the girls get together, they're going to have a good time!

Visit your local Christian bookstore, call NavPress at 1-800-366-7788, or log on to www.navpress.com to purchase.

To locate a Christian bookstore near you, call 1-800-991-7747.